.

INDEX TO

WILLIAMSON COUNTY,

TENNESSEE

WILLS AND ADMINISTRATIONS

1800 – 1861

By

Byron Sistler
and
Barbara Sistler

Originally published, Nashville, 1989

Reprinted with permission by:

Janaway Publishing, Inc.
732 Kelsey Ct.
Santa Maria, California 93454
(805) 925-1038
www.JanawayGenealogy.com

2007, 2011

ISBN: 978-1-59641-061-9

Made in the United States of America

INDEX TO WILLIAMSON COUNTY, TENNESSEE
WILLS AND ADMINISTRATIONS 1800 TO 1861

This index covers all Williamson County, Tennessee, will books from 1800 through 1861. The entries are relatively self-explanatory, but a few observations are in order:

> The year shown is, where possible, the year of the probate; otherwise, the year of the will, or the first year mentioned, relative to the estate.

> At the end of each entry is identification of where the instrument can be found--wb (will book) followed by the book number and the page number. For example, wb-5-267 means will book 5, page 267.

> In general, we attempted to insert a notation regarding an estate only once, when it first appeared in the records. Exceptions were (1) if there was an actual will, the page number was shown even if there was a previous entry for that estate; (2) if a later insertion had been found with a more complete name---name instead of initials, etc.---or a substantially different spelling of what appeared to be the same name; (3) if 10 years or more had passed since the last entry for that name (it might be a different person with the same name).

Guardian proceedings and settlements are to be found sprinkled throughout the books. While these contain much data of genealogical value, we omitted these references as not within the scope of this particular work.

Where a single will book had two series of pagination--starting over with page 1 somewhere in the middle--we have marked the second set of page numbers with an asterisk.

Microfilmed copies of the original books are to be found at the Tennessee State Library and Archives in Nashville.

Byron Sistler
Barbara Sistler

Adams, Jacob 1833 wb-5-267
Adams, James 1859 wb-13-66
Adams, Thomas 1823 wb-3-630
Adams, Wiley 1841 wb-7-487
Adams, Willie 1843 wb-8-128
Aden, Bennett 1858 wb-12-482
Adkins, Amos 1818 wb-2-408
Aikin, Samuel 1844 wb-8-146
Albright, Anna 1853 wb-10-548
Alexander, Susan 1848 wb-9-111
Alexander, Thomas 1855 wb-11-511
Allen, Charles 1848 wb-9-37
Allen, Charles M. 1848 wb-9-62
Allen, F. N. 1853 wb-11-8
Allen, James 1840 wb-7-300
Allen, John 1835 wb-6-55
Allen, John H. 1860 wb-13-173
Allen, John W. 1852 wb-10-404
Allen, Lawson 1861 wb-13-455
Allen, Nancy T. 1845 wb-8-326
Allen, Samuel 1845 wb-8-292
Allen, Sarah Jane 1848 wb-9-185
Allen, Sophronia 1848 wb-9-112
Allen, Theophilus N. 1853 wb-10-458
Allen, William 1852 wb-10-258
Allen, William S. 1844 wb-8-172
Allen, William W. 1849 wb-9-232
Allison, James 1821 Wb-3-243
Allison, Samuel P. 1858 wb-12-542
Allison, William 1834 wb-5-399
Allison, William 1861 wb-13-451
Almond, Elizabeth 1835 wb-6-76
Alston, Edley 1850 wb-9-381
Alston, James 1834 wb-5-365
Alston, James 1857 wb-12-356
Alston, John 1837 wb-6-300
Anderson, Abraham 1816 wb-2-199
Anderson, Elizabeth 1847 wb-8-612
Anderson, James C. 1857 wb-12-460
Anderson, Joel 1850 wb-9-372
Anderson, Robert W. 1852 wb-10-356
Anderson, William C. 1848 wb-9-163
Anderson, William E. 1833 wb-5-281
Andrews, Brockenbrough 1853 wb-11-42
Andrews, Brockenbrough B. 1854 wb-11-103

Andrews, Caroline 1849 wb-9-319

Andrews, Ephraim 1809 wb-1-45

Andrews, Ephraim 1837 wb-6-364

Andrews, Ephraim B. 1847 wb-8-614

Andrews, George 1842 wb-7-547

Andrews, James (or John?) 1850 wb-9-470

Andrews, James 1850 wb-9-584

Andrews, James M. 1839 wb-7-51

Andrews, John 1842 wb-7-534

Andrews, John 1842 wb-7-547

Andrews, Jones 1844 wb-8-135

Andrews, Mark 1821 wb-3-211

Andrews, Mark 1831 wb-5-40

Andrews, Mark L. 1851 wb-10-132

Andrews, R. L. 1839 wb-7-33

Andrews, Richard L. 1839 wb-7-91

Andrews, Samuel M. 1860 wb-13-174

Andrews, Stith H. 1856 wb-12-50

Andrews, Thomas 1852 wb-10-168

Andrews, William 1829 wb-4-459

Andrews, Winnefred 1827 wb-4-243

Anthony, Sarah 1853 wb-10-499

Anthony, William 1847 wb-9-1

Appleby, William 1808 wb-1-37

Applewhite, Charlotte 1838 wb-7-5

Armstrong, James 1834 wb-5-427

Armstrong, Mary 1846 wb-8-452

Armstrong, William sr. 1846 wb-8-453

Ashlin, Dicey 1847 wb-8-604

Ashlin, William 1821 Wb-3-272

Atkins, John 1813 wb-2-8

Atkins, Thomas S. 1817 wb-2-278

Atkinson, Elizabeth 1855 wb-12-1

Atkinson, John 1814 Wb-2-57

Atkinson, John 1837 wb-6-324

Atkinson, Ruthy J. 1860 wb-13-179

Attkisson, Ruth 1829 wb-4-459

Austin, Polly 1833 wb-5-306

Austin, Raleigh 1832 wb-5-159

Bailey, Henry 1834 wb-5-440

Bailey, John H. 1839 wb-7-204

Baily, Henry 1835 wb-6-66

Balance, Sarah 1826 wb-4-110

Ballance, Abraham 1825 wb-4-31

Ballard, Thomas 1813 wb-1-340

Ballow, Ann F. 1854 wb-11-160

Ballow, James 1853 wb-10-593

Ballow, Thomas 1813 wb-2-25

Banks, James M. 1835 wb-6-70

Banks, James M. 1850 wb-9-425

Barfield, Nancy 1830 wb-4-497

Barfield, Stephen 1818 wb-2-378

Barham, William P. 1850 wb-9-379

Barker, George W. 1860 wb-13-227

Barnes, George 1852 wb-10-419

Barnes, Nancy 1858 wb-12-603

Barnes, Nathaniel 1816 wb-2-220

Barnes, Susanna 1815 Wb-2-175

Barnett, E. E. 1857 wb-12-478

Barnett, James P. 1827 wb-4-202

Bartlett, George 1848 wb-9-193

Bass, Kinchen P. 1818 wb-2-374

Bateman, Enoch 1846 wb-8-401

Bateman, Evan 1842 wb-7-566

Bateman, Henry W. 1856 wb-12-187

Bateman, Isaac 1833 wb-5-269

Bateman, Jonathan 1818 wb-2-377

Bateman, Parker 1815 Wb-2-167

Bateman, William 1843 wb-8-1

Baugh, Daniel 1857 wb-12-407

Baugh, James 1843 wb-8-68

Baugh, Philip W. 1860 wb-13-337

Baugh, Wyatt W. 1860 wb-13-172

Beale, James W. 1849 wb-9-161

Beale, Richard 1859 wb-13-163

Beard, Bird N. 1858 wb-13-9

Beard, John 1826 wb-4-113

Beard, Mary 1853 wb-11-82

Beasley, John P. 1848 wb-9-202

Beasley, Philip 1819 wb-3-102

Beasley, Robert E. 1814 Wb-2-76

Beasley, Zachariah 1840 wb-7-249

Beatty, Henry 1846 wb-8-513

Beech, Elizabeth B. 1841 wb-7-475

Beech, James B. 1846 wb-8-396

Beech, John B. 1830 wb-4-542

Beech, Lodowick B. 1841 wb-7-466

Beech, Lodwick B. 1850 wb-9-353

Beech, Peter S. 1856 wb-12-77

Beech, Sarah 1859 wb-13-84

Belew, Thomas 1816 wb-2-206

Bell, Nathaniel 1848 wb-9-174

Bell, William jr. 1803 wb-1-8

Bell, William R. 1816 wb-2-218

Benbrook, John 1830 wb-4-541

Bennett, George 1823 wb-3-601

Bennett, George W. 1861 wb-13-418

Bennett, Joseph W. 1859 wb-13-118

Bennett, Walter 1814 Wb-2-79

Bennett, William L. 1841 wb-7-485

Benson, John 1815 Wb-2-130

Benton, Jessee 1812 Wb-2-91

Benton, John 1814 Wb-2-107

Benton, Nancy 1807 wb-1-28

Berry, James 1814 Wb-2-105

Berry, Leanard L. T. 1838 wb-6-470

Berry, Thomas 1844 wb-8-205

Berry, Thomas S. 1836 wb-6-158

Berry, William 1810 wb-1-222

Betty, Henry 1849 wb-9-243

Betty, William H. 1833 wb-5-220

Biggar, Joseph 1833 wb-5-268

Biggar, Katharine 1852 wb-10-168

Biggar, Robert 1820 wb-3-178

Biggar, Thomas 1828 wb-4-356

Biggars, Martha 1824 wb-3-703

Billow, James 1856 wb-12-94

Bingham, Thomas 1854 wb-11-317

Binghqm, Franklin M. 1839 wb-7-28

Bittick, Samuel F. 1853 wb-10-484

Bizzell, James 1855 wb-11-512

Black, William 1836 wb-6-88

Blackburn, Andrew D. 1856 wb-12-242

Blackshare, Jesse 1803 Wb-1-116

Blackwell, Thomas 1858 wb-12-493

Bland, Arthur 1816 wb-2-215

Blythe, Elizabeth 1861 wb-13-469

Blythe, James 1829 wb-4-381

Blythe, John 1834 wb-5-384

Blythe, William 1825 wb-4-13

Bobbett, Stephen 1831 wb-5-47

Bond, Elizabeth M. 1855 wb-11-433

Bond, Isabella M. E. 1855 wb-11-486

Bond, James 1851 wb-10-1

Bond, James B. 1851 wb-10-28

Bond, James M. 1854 wb-11-404

Bond, John B. 1848 wb-9-169

Bond, John H. 1854 wb-11-97

Bond, Margarett L. 1852 wb-10-169

Bond, Morris L. 1825 wb-3-768

Bond, Nancy M. 1861 wb-13-439

Bond, Sarah C. 1857 wb-12-422

Bond, Thomas B. 1848 wb-9-112

Bond, Thomas J. 1848 wb-9-111

Bond, William 1820 wb-3-119

Bond, William 1829 wb-4-457

Bond, William 1850 wb-9-469

Bond, William W. 1856 wb-12-63

Boon, Amelia 1849 wb-9-286

Bostick, Hanoah 1837 wb-6-347

Bostick, John 1850 wb-9-354

Bostick, John jr. 1855 wb-11-446

Bostick, John sr. 1850 wb-9-449

Bostick, Manoah 1837 wb-6-374

Bostick, R. W. H. 1853 wb-11-41

Bostick, Richard W. H. 1854 wb-11-93

Boyd, America A. 1827 wb-4-228

Boyd, Armstead 1815 wb-2-151

Boyd, George G. 1841 wb-7-465

Boyd, Harrison 1818 wb-2-378

Boyd, James 1821 Wb-3-248

Boyd, James W. 1847 wb-8-593

Boyd, John R. 1819 wb-3-103

Boyd, Martha 1843 wb-8-40

Boyd, Mary 1845 wb-8-246

Boyd, Washington L. 1860 wb-13-168

Boyd, William G. 1841 wb-7-464

Boyd, William J. 1829 wb-4-366

Bradley, James H. 1861 wb-13-421

Bradley, Leland J. 1861 wb-13-457

Bradley, Stephen S. 1853 wb-10-610

Bradley, Thomas 1849 wb-9-288

Bragg, Moore 1816 wb-2-212

Branch, Joseph 1827 wb-4-253

Branch, Joseph 1834 wb-5-371

Branckler, Daniel 1846 wb-8-379

Brantley, Hannah M. 1852 wb-10-190

Brantley, J. M. (Mrs.) 1852 wb-10-206

Brickle, James 1841 wb-7-435

Bridges, William 1806 wb-1-155

Briggs, Sterling 1858 wb-12-584

Brim, John 1848 wb-9-129

Brockler, Daniel 1845 wb-8-365

Brooks, Amanda 1849 wb-9-296

Brooks, Christopher 1832 wb-5-135

Brooks, Elijah 1827 wb-4-213

Brooks, Elijah G. 1849 wb-9-302

Brooks, George 1836 wb-6-279

Brooks, George A. 1849 wb-9-248

Brooks, George Magdalen K. 1841 wb-7-457

Brooks, Hannah 1841 wb-7-466

Brooks, James 1827 wb-4-155

Brooks, John 1842 wb-7-585

Brooks, Priscilla 1845 wb-8-355

Broomfield, Elisha 1841 wb-7-468

Browder, Fredrick 1815 wb-2-158

Browder, Rhoda 1838 wb-6-456

Brown, Benjamin 1836 wb-6-116

Brown, Charles 1816 wb-2-230

Brown, Ephraim 1841 wb-7-366

Brown, Henry 1852 wb-10-212

Brown, James P. 1852 wb-10-415

Brown, John E. 1846 wb-8-481

Brown, Joseph 1814 Wb-2-96

Brown, Joseph A. 1858 wb-12-557

Brown, Littleton 1815 Wb-2-145

Brown, Nancy 1847 wb-8-535

Brown, Nathaniel 1814 Wb-2-99

Brown, Nathaniel 1836 wb-6-109

Brown, Ruffin 1838 wb-6-515

Brown, Samuel 1848 wb-9-181

Brown, Spencer H. 1837 wb-6-295

Brown, Susan 1833 wb-5-294

Brown, Susan 1845 wb-8-283

Brown, Susannah 1841 wb-7-374

Brown, Theoderick C. 1842 wb-7-511

Brown, Thomas C. 1840 wb-7-286

Brown, William 1840 wb-7-321

Brown, William 1856 wb-12-219

Brown, William H. 1828 wb-4-282

Brown, William M. 1847 wb-8-595

Brownlee, James 1827 wb-4-262

Buchanan, Eleanor 1858 wb-12-609

Buchanan, John 1849 wb-9-287

Buchannan, John 1834 wb-5-394

Buchanon, John 1820 wb-3-198

Buck, Mary 1854 wb-11-364

Buck, Mary W. 1855 wb-11-434

Buck, Peter S. 1861 wb-13-388

Buckhanan, John 1848 wb-9-204

Buckingham, James 1831 wb-5-14

Buford, Edward 1828 wb-4-332

Buford, Edward 1842 wb-7-573

Buford, Emily R. 1841 wb-7-361

Buford, James 1811 wb-1-255

Buford, John R. 1851 wb-9-663

Buford, Mary W. 1857 wb-12-366

Buford, Mary W. 1858 wb-12-529

Buford, Robert 1852 wb-10-431

Buford, Robert J. 1856 wb-12-130

Buford, Spencer 1845 wb-8-301

Bugg, Allen 1828 wb-4-279

Bugg, Allen 1836 wb-6-125

Bugg, Benjamin 1813 wb-1-318

Bugg, Ephraim M. W. 1846 wb-8-371

Bullock, William 1808 wb-1-43

Bulls, Barnaby 1822 wb-3-321

Burch, Elizabeth 1829 wb-4-392

Burch, John 1827 wb-4-195

Burge, Henry A. 1826 wb-4-144

Burge, Mary 1837 wb-6-331

Burgess, James 1830 wb-4-493

Burgess, Rhoda 1855 wb-12-9

Burgess, William 1854 wb-11-363

Burk, John 1857 wb-12-409

Burke, Anson 1841 wb-7-407

Burke, William 1859 wb-13-207

Burnett, Joseph 1849 wb-9-314

Burnett, Tolefor 1822 wb-3-363

Burnham, Mary 1853 wb-10-530

Butler, Polly 1857 wb-12-406

Butler, Thomas 1846 wb-8-379

Buttrey, John 1857 wb-12-443

Butts, Sarah 1858 wb-12-547

Byers, Elizabeth C. 1859 wb-13-67

Byers, Isabella E. 1841 wb-7-434

Byers, James 1858 wb-12-587

Byers, William 1837 wb-6-368

Byers, William 1837 wb-7-25

Byers, William 1851 wb-10-117

Byers, William 1851 wb-10-31

Byrd, Baylor 1830 wb-4-544

Cahoon, Charles 1823 wb-3-634

Caldwell, Andrew B. 1847 wb-8-534

Caldwell, Rachael E. 1850 wb-9-376

Caldwell, Thos. G. 1810 wb-1-226

Calhoun, Robert W. 1841 wb-7-375

Calhoun, Wilson W. 1839 wb-7-30

Cameron, Ewen 1846 wb-8-415

Cameron, Ewen 1853 wb-11-27

Campbell, Andrew 1818 wb-2-414

Campbell, Andrew 1831 wb-5-53

Campbell, Edward 1826 wb-4-84

Campbell, Jane B. 1825 wb-4-3

Campbell, John 1808 wb-1-178

Camron, Polly S. 1835 wb-6-79

Cannon, Letitia 1832 wb-5-154

Cannon, Minos 1829 wb-4-434

Caperton, Susan 1856 wb-12-100

Caperton, Thompson 1855 wb-12-9

Capps, Polly 1853 wb-10-594

Cardle, Eliz. 1846 wb-8-358

Carl, Jacob 1845 wb-8-302

Carl, Jacob 1857 wb-12-396

Carl, Jacob B. 1854 wb-11-90

Carlile, Robert 1809 wb-1-199

Carmichael, Archibald 1859 wb-13-165

Carothers, James D. 1840 wb-7-328

Carothers, James L. 1860 wb-13-233

Carothers, Martha S. 1856 wb-12-284

Carrol, Jesse 1820 wb-3-124

Carsey, Sarah A. 1851 wb-10-63

Carsey, Thomas P. 1836 wb-6-227

Carsey, William P. 1847 wb-8-610

Carson, James 1845 wb-8-253

Carson, John 1826 wb-4-94

Carson, Joseph 1834 wb-5-343

Carson, Joseph 1834 wb-5-375

Carson, Martha A. 1852 wb-10-269

Carson, Robert 1855 wb-11-509

Carson, Samuel 1815 Wb-2-172

Carson, William 1851 wb-10-137

Carson, Willis 1815 Wb-2-176

Carter, Daniel 1844 wb-8-175

Carter, Isaac 1823 wb-3-607

Carter, James F. 1859 wb-13-146

Carter, Newton 1848 wb-9-159

Carter, Richard 1815 Wb-2-146

Carter, Robert 1839 wb-7-207

Carter, Sarah 1852 wb-10-218

Carter, Theodrick 1839 wb-7-32

Cartwright, David 1860 wb-13-215

Cartwright, David 1860 wb-13-286

Cash, Elisha 1802 Wb-1-97

Cash, Thomas 1829 wb-4-437

Cate, William H. 1823 wb-3-666

Cathey, George 1835 wb-6-50

Cator, Levin 1848 wb-9-69

Cator, Martha 1839 wb-7-27

Cator, Moses E. sr. 1853 wb-11-45

Chadwell, Valentine 1831 wb-5-1

Champ, John 1810 wb-1-223

Champ, John 1821 Wb-3-242

Chaney, Ezekiel 1840 wb-7-223

Chaney, H. W. 1858 wb-12-599

Chaney, Houston W. 1860 wb-13-241

Chaney, W. T. 1850 wb-9-594

Chaney, Wilkins T. 1852 wb-10-445

Chaney, William T. 1850 wb-9-602

Chaplin, Elizabeth 1844 wb-8-177

Chaplin, Elizabeth M. 1845 wb-8-245

Chapman, Benjamin 1846 wb-8-482

Chapman, Elizabeth 1856 wb-12-288

Charter, John 0. P. 1843 wb-8-74

Charter, John N. 1848 wb-9-39

Cherry, W. N. 1861 wb-13-439

Cherry, William 1860 wb-13-262

Childress, Henry 1814 Wb-2-42

Childress, Thomas M. 1829 wb-4-432

Childress, William G. 1846 wb-8-477

Chriesman, Mary 1854 wb-11-182

Chrisman, Abraham 1822 wb-3-593

Chrisman, Aron 1817 wb-2-309

Chrisman, James J. 1860 wb-13-322

Chrisman, Samuel S. 1861 wb-13-453

Christman, David 1841 wb-7-373

Christmas, Abraham 1822 wb-3-586

Christmas, William 1812 wb-1-264

Christmas, William 1822 wb-3-352

Chriswell, Abel 1851 wb-9-673

Chriswell, Andrew 1842 wb-7-559

Chriswell, Martha F. 1853 wb-10-597

Chriswelll, Laban 1857 wb-12-384

Church, Thomas 1849 wb-9-288

Clark, Samuel 1807 wb-1-166

Clark, Samuel 1818 wb-2-377

Clark, William 1841 wb-7-477

Claud, Eldridge 1848 wb-9-118

Claud, Joshua D. 1836 wb-6-276

Claud, Philip 1848 wb-9-32

Claud, Susan 1854 wb-11-257

Clay, Green 1851 wb-10-36

Clemm, James S. 1826 wb-4-143

Cochran, John 1825 wb-4-1

Cochran, John 1856 wb-12-219

Cochran, Susan 1856 wb-12-189

Coddington, Benjamin 1803 Wb-1-91

Codey, William 1857 wb-12-298

Cohoon, George 1820 wb-3-177

Cole, Joseph 1810 wb-1-214

Cole, Thomas 1815 Wb-2-164

Cole, Thomas 1827 wb-4-278

Cole, William 1822 wb-3-341

Coleman, Elizabeth 1832 wb-5-133

Coleman, Jones R. 1844 wb-8-187

Coleman, Joseph 1857 wb-12-386

Coleman, Joshua 1821 Wb-3-271

Coleman, Sutton 1858 wb-12-492

Colhoon, Charles 1822 wb-3-587

Collins, Hodijah 1826 wb-4-145

Collins, Thomas 1851 wb-10-41

Coltart, William 1840 wb-7-340

Comstock, Clark M. 1861 wb-13-561

Cook, Edmund 1809 Wb-1-54

Cook, Gracey B. 1851 wb-9-654

Cook, Henry 1833 wb-5-319

Cook, John 1834 wb-5-396

Cook, John T. 1848 wb-9-196

Cook, John Z. 1846 wb-8-432

Cook, Joseph S. 1839 wb-7-31

Cooper, D. H. 1854 wb-11-391

Coor, Thomas 1816 wb-2-219

Coore, James H. 1824 wb-3-688

Copeland, James 1817 wb-3-81

Cordel, Elizabeth 1846 wb-8-410

Core, William C. 1840 wb-0-326

Corlett, Robert 1827 wb-4-229

Corzine, Abel 1828 wb-4-343

Corzine, Abel 1842 wb-0-522

Corzine, Eli 1821 Wb-3-255

Corzine, Rees 1839 wb-0-106

Courtney, Robert 1859 wb-13-167

Cowan, David A. 1853 wb-10-599

Cowan, Joseph 1846 wb-8-392

Cowan, Sarah H. 1846 wb-8-490

Cowls, Jesse 1861 wb-13-423

Cowsert, Andrew 1824 wb-3-722

Cowsert, Jane 1832 wb-5-158

Cox, Daniel 1802 Wb-1-99

Cox, Garner M. 1852 wb-10-193

Cox, George R. 1840 wb-7-216

Cox, Nancy 1859 wb-13-109

Craddock, Martha G. 1838 wb-6-444

Craddock, Matthew R. 1836 wb-6-113

Crafton, James 1810 wb-1-209

Crafton, John 1816 wb-2-220

Craig, David 1812 wb-1-320

Craig, David 1820 wb-4-204

Craig, David 1825 wb-4-2

Craig, Mary 1826 wb-4-149

Craige, Daniel 1828 wb-4-350

Crawford, John 1813 wb-1-341

Creecy, Nancy 1829 wb-4-385

Crenshaw, Cornelius 1810 wb-2-262

Crenshaw, John 1813 wb-2-9

Crenshaw, John C. 1810 wb-2-323

Crenshaw, Nathaniel 1859 wb-13-00

Crenshaw, Sarah 1860 wb-13-283

Crichiow, Henry E. 1860 wb-13-449

Crichlow, Henry 1858 wb-12-596

Criddle, Alexander E. 1846 wb-8-300

Criddle, James 1861 wb-13-401

Criddle, James M. 1861 wb-13-480

Cristman, James 1860 wb-13-280

Criswell, Andrew 1837 wb-6-408

Critz, Jacob 1821 Wb-3-228

Critz, James M. 1852 wb-10-190

Critz, John C. 1834 wb-5-362

Critz, John C. 1836 wb-6-114

Crocket, Andrew 1838 wb-0-18

Crockett, Abraham 1828 wb-4-285

Crockett, Andrew 1821 Wb-3-246

Crockett, Andrew 1852 wb-10-383

Crockett, John H. 1828 wb-4-289

Crockett, John H. 1842 wb-0-523

Crockett, Joseph 1853 wb-10-526

Crockett, Nancy 1844 wb-8-168

Crockett, Samuel 1820 wb-4-199

Crosby, Levi 1839 wb-0-95

Crouch, John 1814 Wb-2-66

Crow, Isaac 1813 wb-2-32

Crow, Joanna 1822 wb-3-571

Crowder, Bartholomew 1854 wb-11-161

Crowder, William J. 1831 wb-5-81

Crum, Eliza P. 1842 wb-7-590

Crump, Findal 1824 wb-3-701

Crump, John 0. 1849 wb-9-320

Crutcher, Nancy 1844 wb-8-155

Crutcher, Preston L. 1845 wb-8-366

Crutcher, Willis 1844 wb-8-138

Culbert, George 1823 wb-3-660

Cumins, Samuel 1832 wb-5-202

Cummins, David 1836 wb-6-200

Cummins, Henry 1838 wb-7-3

Cummins, Waller 1848 wb-9-43

Cunningham, James A. 1852 wb-10-368

Cunningham, John P. 1835 wb-6-26

Currin, Barsheba 1857 wb-12-464

Currin, John M. 1852 wb-10-389

Curtis, Aaron D. 1825 wb-3-766

Curtis, Benjamin 1827 wb-4-211

Curtis, Benjamin 1828 wb-4-299

Dabney, Charles A. 1830 wb-4-402

Dabney, John 1831 wb-5-21

Dabney, Mary E. 1837 wb-6-298

Dabney, William 1828 wb-4-338

Dabney, William 1828 wb-4-351

Dalton, John 1858 wb-12-539

Daniel, Edward 1854 wb-11-319

Davenport, Hughston 1831 wb-5-02

Davis, Ammon 1807 wb-1-20

Davis, Charles F. 1848 wb-9-90

Davis, David 1805 Wb-1-126

Davis, Elisha 1836 wb-6-153

Davis, Fredrick 1831 wb-5-75

Davis, George 1849 wb-9-220

Davis, Harvy 1847 wb-8-561

Davis, Holcome 1836 wb-6-118

Davis, Hollon 1836 wb-6-163

Davis, Hollon 1836 wb-6-259

Davis, James R. 1830 wb-6-358

Davis, Jonathan 1808 wb-1-182

Davis, Louisa F. 1852 wb-10-234

Davis, Mary 1845 wb-8-300

Davis, Nathaniel 1843 wb-8-40

Davis, Robert 1838 wb-0-58

Davis, Sally 1828 wb-4-344

Davis, Sarah 1839 wb-0-135

Davis, Seth F. 1850 wb-9-394

Davis, Seth L. 1860 wb-13-325

Davis, Seth T. 1847 wb-8-560

Davis, Sterling 1856 wb-12-202

Davis, Stokely A. 1847 wb-8-562

Davis, Turner 1861 wb-13-402

Davis, William 1808 wb-1-179

Davis, Wilson 1839 wb-7-53

Davis, Wilson B. 1839 wb-7-59

Dean, Francis 1829 wb-4-445

Dean, Richard 1827 wb-4-159

Degraffenreid, Matcalf 1803 Wb-1-111

Degraffenreid, Metcalf 1806 wb-3-67

DeGraffenried, Metcalf 1839 wb-7-183

Dempsey, Hugh 1849 wb-9-227

Devorix, William C. 1815 Wb-2-130

Devoux, William C. 1814 Wb-2-109

Dial, James 1825 wb-4-30

Dickens, John 1808 wb-1-30

Dobbins, Jane 1842 wb-7-489

Dobbins, William 1831 wb-5-43

Dobson, Henry 1824 wb-3-702

Dodd, Henry P. 1846 wb-8-487

Dodd, Jane 1843 wb-8-101

Dodd, Samuel 1837 wb-6-399

Dodd, Serena 1842 wb-7-556

Dodd, Wilkins 1848 wb-9-164

Dodson, John R. 1855 wb-11-504

Dodson, Mary 1854 wb-11-116

Dodson, Presley 1840 wb-7-222

Dodson, Presley 1850 wb-9-393

Dodson, Rawley 1836 wb-6-247

Doherty, Mary 1836 wb-6-208

Doil, Kintchen 1815 Wb-2-136

Dollar, William 1832 wb-5-178

Donelson, Lemuel 1833 wb-5-229

Donnelson, Robert 1837 wb-6-409

Dortch, Willis R. 1858 wb-13-4

Dotson, Hightower 1823 wb-3-613

Dotson, Unity 1827 wb-4-174

Douglass, Thomas L. 1843 wb-8-45

Dowd, John 1812 wb-1-283

Dowdy, John 1845 wb-8-282

Downey, William 1823 wb-3-616

Downing, Milton H. 1847 wb-9-25

Doyle, Michael 1843 wb-8-10

Drake, James L. 1858 wb-12-607

Drake, Rhoda 1839 wb-7-186

Drake, Zachariah 1822 wb-3-297

Dudley, Guilford 1833 wb-5-264

Dunaway, James G. 1837 wb-6-359

Duncan, A. B. 1857 wb-12-480

Dunham, John 1817 wb-2-359

Dupree, James 1819 wb-3-102

Dyer, John 1818 wb-2-390

Early, Harriet J. 1860 wb-13-224

Early, Joshua 1860 wb-13-338

Eastep, Samuel 1836 wb-6-225

Eastwood, Esquire 1857 wb-12-393

Eaton, Elizabeth 1843 wb-8-110

Eaton, John 1817 wb-2-364

Echols, Frances 1840 wb-7-314

Echols, John 1816? wb-2-304

Edgar, John 1843 wb-8-64

Edmiston, James E. 1815 wb-2-150

Edmiston, John 1824 wb-3-673

Edmiston, John 1839 wb-7-182

Edmiston, John B. 1844 wb-8-159

Edmiston, Samuel 1821 Wb-3-263

Edmonds, William 1850 wb-9-437

Edmondson, John 1827 wb-4-165

Edmondson, William 1832 wb-5-182

Edmondson, William 1844 wb-8-193

Edmonston, Andrew J. 1855 wb-11-499

Edney, Alson 1816 wb-2-270

Edney, Polly 1824 wb-3-700

Edwards, John 1822 wb-3-329

Edwards, John N. 1858 wb-12-592

Edwards, Susan 1848 wb-9-184

Edwards, William 1850 wb-9-465

Elam, Edward 1830 wb-4-492

Elam, Edward 1846 wb-8-436

Elam, Jane 1846 wb-8-434

Elam, Stephen 1813 wb-2-9

Elliot, Knacy H. 1840 wb-7-243

Elliott, Alexander N. 1852 wb-10-261

Elliott, Allen 1848 wb-9-205

Elliott, Exum 1827 wb-4-233

Elliott, Joseph M. C. 1837 wb-6-396

Elliott, Knacey 1838 wb-6-469

Ellis, George T. 1848 wb-9-178

Ellis, James 1840 wb-7-295

Ellis, Wyatt 1855 wb-11-565

Epperson, Littleberry 1812 wb-1-288

Eppes, Elizabeth 1840 wb-7-304

Epps, George 1849 wb-9-294

Epps, Peter 1841 wb-7-425

Erwin, David 1826 wb-4-127

Evans, Ann 1847 wb-8-533

Evans, Benjamin 1820 wb-3-123

Evans, Isham 1814 Wb-2-107

Evans, Jesse 1805 wb-1-14

Evans, Jesse 1830 wb-4-499

Evans, John 1856 wb-12-206

Evans, John jr. 1853 wb-11-69

Evans, John jr. 1856 wb-12-255

Evans, John sr. 1851 wb-9-660

Evans, John W. 1850 wb-9-593

Evans, Martha 1812 wb-1-282

Everly, Jacob 1836 wb-6-128

Evins, David 1814 Wb-2-78

Ewing, Alexander 1850 wb-9-447

Ewing, Alexander C. 1834 wb-5-393

Ewing, Chloe R. 1839 wb-7-162

Ezell, Balaam 1833 wb-5-295

Ezell, Balaam 1850 wb-9-387

Ezell, Frederick 1859 wb-13-36

Ezell, Jeremiah 1852 wb-10-374

Farmer, Jane 1857 wb-12-468

Farmer, Moses E. 1841 wb-7-468

Farrar, William James 1857 wb-12-461

Fergus, James 1806 wb-3-69

Ferguson, David S. 1843 wb-8-10

Ferguson, Joel 1841 wb-7-409

Fields, Bennett 1818 wb-2-379

Fields, Nelson 1839 wb-7-94

Figuers, Thomas N. 1854 wb-11-243

Fisher, Eli A. 1839 wb-7-200

Fittz, Ulysses 1841 wb-7-376

Fitzgerald, John Sr. 1858 wb-12-499

Fleming, David B. 1859 wb-13-65

Fleming, James 1826 wb-4-143

Fleming, Josiah 1853 wb-11-80

Fleming, Ralph 1821 Wb-3-258

Flippin, Jacob 1839 wb-7-122

Flippin, Robert 1853 wb-11-35

Floyd, Jones 1857 wb-12-331

Floyd, Josiah 1850 wb-9-378

Forehand, John 1837 wb-6-385

Foster, Shelton C. 1836 wb-6-132

Fowlkes, Nancy Jane 1857 wb-12-401

Fox, Elijah 1861 wb-13-589

Fox, Hugh 1841 wb-7-460

Fox, Hugh 1853 wb-11-44

Frances, Moses B. 1819 wb-3-104

Frantham, John R. 1851 wb-10-2

Freeman, Arthur 1809 Wb-1-85

Freeman, John 1839 wb-7-93

French, Lewis H. 1857 wb-12-462

Frost, John 1836 wb-6-228

Fry, Joseph H. 1837 wb-6-396

Furguson, Mary F. 1859 wb-13-139

Gambling, John 1808 wb-1-180

Gant, Benjamin R. 1853 wb-10-547

Gardner, Jane 1808 wb-1-33

Gardner, Jane 1818 wb-2-388

Gardner, Jane 1819 wb-3-15

Gardner, John 1856 wb-12-231

Gardner, William 1806 wb-1-19

Gardner, William 1819 wb-3-1

Garey, James 1852 wb-10-271

Garnett, James H. 1853 wb-10-502

Garrett, Caleb 1841 wb-7-478

Garrett, Henry 1845 wb-8-346

Garrett, Jane 1818 wb-2-392

Garrett, John 1806 wb-1-139

Garrett, Thomas 1837 wb-6-329

Gary, James 1847 wb-9-8

Gault, James 1837 wb-6-399

Gay, James 1806 wb-1-145

Gee, Mary W. 1847 wb-9-9

Gee, Nelson W. 1859 wb-13-69

Gee, William 0. 1843 wb-8-52

Gentry, Reuben A. 1841 wb-7-435

Gentry, Ruth T. 1852 wb-10-525

Gentry, Samuel R. 1816 wb-2-231

Gentry, Thomas G. 1833 wb-5-280

Gentry, Watson 1844 wb-8-167

German, Daniel sr. 1859 wb-13-24

German, Elizabeth 1824 wb-3-719

German, Elizabeth 1827 wb-4-235

German, Joseph 1819 wb-3-1

Gholson, John 1817 wb-2-334

Gibson, James 1831 wb-5-58

Gibson, John B. 1824 wb-3-742

Gibson, Partrick 1850 wb-9-384

Gibson, Patrick 1817 wb-2-291

Gibson, Sarah A. 1846 wb-8-491

Giddens, Francis sr. 1830 wb-4-531

Giles, Edward 1858 wb-12-504

Giles, Edward J. 1857 wb-12-401

Giles, Josiah E. 1828 wb-4-309

Giles, Newton C. 1856 wb-12-226

Giles, Patrick G. 1846 wb-8-452

Giles, Robertson 1851 wb-10-47

Giles, William 1844 wb-8-193

Gill, Caleb T. 1834 wb-5-358

Gillaspie, David A. 1861 wb-13-488

Gillaspie, Isaac 1828 wb-4-349

Gillaspie, James 1807 wb-3-65

Gillespie, David 1861 wb-13-438

Gillespie, George 1834 wb-5-448

Gillespie, Isaac 1828 wb-4-310

Gillespie, Mary 1846 wb-8-397

Gillespie, Robert 1851 wb-10-94

Gillespie, Thomas 1830 wb-4-533

Gilliam, Anthony 1851 wb-10-119

Gillispie, David 1835 wb-6-67

Gillispie, George 1834 wb-6-17

Gillispie, George A. 1836 wb-6-44

Givens, Henry R. 1854 wb-11-313

Glass, Robert 1850 wb-9-451

Glenn, Abram 1851 wb-10-30

Glenn, William 1836 wb-6-184

Glimph, George 1829 wb-4-433

Glover, Jones 1803 Wb-1-105

Glover, Jones 1806 wb-3-78

Gocey, James 1854 wb-11-365

Gocey, Lew? R. 1847 wb-8-559

Goff, Andrew 1827 wb-4-260

Goff, Andrew 1831 wb-5-74

Goff, Andrew 1849 wb-9-228

Goff, James 1850 wb-9-355

Goff, Thomas 1817 wb-2-345

Goff, William 1849 wb-9-308

Gooch, David 1831 wb-5-70

Gooch, David 1844 wb-8-144

Gooch, Edward J. 1851 wb-10-137

Gooch, Thomas 1817 wb-2-342

Gooch, William 1852 wb-10-210

Goodman, Benijah 1820 wb-3-179

Goodrum, Allen 1822 wb-3-293

Goodrum, Jane 1825 wb-4-17

Goodrum, Thomas 1825 wb-4-13

Gordon, Thomas 1821 Wb-3-271

Gosey, Rebecca 1860 wb-13-290

Gowen, William 1816 wb-2-192

Graham, Francis 1831 wb-5-62

Graham, John 1836 wb-6-118

Graham, John H. 1848 wb-9-118

Graham, Richard 1833 wb-5-279

Graham, Robert 1829 wb-4-468

Gray, Hardy P. 1845 wb-8-258

Gray, Henry H. 1852 wb-10-428

Gray, James 1809 wb-1-48

Gray, John 1828 wb-4-296

Gray, John 1838 wb-7-1

Gray, Mary J. 1861 wb-13-391

Gray, Price 1855 wb-11-506

Gray, Sally L. R. 1813 wb-1-336

Grear, Mary 1824 wb-3-723

Green, Henry R. 1854 wb-11-262

Green, Lewis 1845 wb-8-248

Green, Priscilla 1855 wb-11-575

Green, Sherwood 1840 wb-7-292

Green, William 1809 wb-1-40

Greer, Mary 1850 wb-9-366

Gregory, John 1841 wb-7-362

Gremmer, Dorcas M. 1852 wb-10-194

Gremmer, Jacob 1843 wb-8-123

Gremmer, Jacob 1844 wb-8-135

Griffon, Nathaniel 1837 wb-6-326

Griggs, Thomas J. 1854 wb-11-191

Griggs, Thomas J. 1856 wb-12-210

Grimes, James 1836 wb-6-276

Gulley, Jesse 1814 Wb-2-107

Gunter, Frances 1850 wb-9-397

Gunter, Francis 1840 wb-7-278

Guthrie, David C. 1833 wb-5-271

Guthrie, David H. 1833 wb-5-229

Guthrie, Robert 1838 wb-6-492

Guthrie, Sally V. 1843 wb-8-86

Guy, John 1824 wb-3-745

Guy, John W. 1832 wb-5-121

Hadley, James H. 1836 wb-6-217

Haffy, Hugh 1842 wb-7-582

Hairgrove, Bennett 1854 wb-11-371

Hairgrove, David B. 1854 wb-11-258

Haithcock, D. A. 1853 wb-10-526

Haithcock, Dempsey A. 1855 wb-11-490

Haley, Banister 1848 wb-9-176

Haley, Overton 1846 wb-8-462

Haley, Richard 1843 wb-8-1

Haley, Wyatt 1848 wb-9-72

Halfacre, Andrew 1836 wb-6-116

Halfacre, David 1848 wb-9-40

Halfacre, David 1859 wb-13-180

Halfacre, Elizabeth 1836 wb-6-102

Halfacre, Elizabeth 1857 wb-12-421

Halfacre, Henry 1854 wb-11-162

Halfacre, Jacob 1849 wb-9-318

Halfacre, Jacob 1859 wb-13-80

Halfacre, Tom 1855 wb-11-486

Hall, Anderson 1849 wb-9-299

Hall, Joseph 1815 wb-2-153

Hall, Robert P. 1826 wb-4-112

Hall, Thomas 1830 wb-4-494

Ham, Jesse 1846 wb-8-454

Hamer, Daniel H. 1840 wb-7-307

Hamer, Emily H. 1858 wb-13-4

Hamer, Harris H. 1858 wb-13-26

Hamer, Miranda 1849 wb-9-307

Hamilton, Elijah 1826 wb-4-68

Hamilton, John W. 1829 wb-4-439

Hamilton, Martha L. 1830 wb-4-515

Hamilton, Mary 1830 wb-4-476

Hamilton, Milton S. 1834 wb-5-398

Hamilton, Nancy 1833 wb-5-337

Hamilton, William S. 1829 wb-4-379

Hampton, David 1841 wb-7-377

Hampton, Elizabeth 1839 wb-7-139

Hampton, Elizabeth 1850 wb-9-410

Hampton, Henry 1858 wb-12-585

Hampton, Jeremiah 1824 wb-3-673

Hampton, Jerry 1838 wb-6-476

Hampton, Nancy 1851 wb-10-161

Hampton, Robert C. 1832 wb-5-184

Hampton, Rufus S. 1854 wb-11-304

Hampton, Sarah Jane 1858 wb-13-8

Hampton, William 1829 wb-4-434

Hardeman, Bailey 1838 wb-6-506

Hardeman, George W. L. 1836 wb-6-242

Hardeman, Nicholas P. 1818 wb-2-387

Hardeman, Nicholas W. 1845 wb-8-343

Hardeman, Peter 1820 wb-3-193

Hardeman, Seth L. 1830 wb-4-537

Hardeman, Thomas 1836 wb-6-270

Harden, Jeremiah 1829 wb-4-365

Harder, John N. 1819 wb-3-3

Harder, John N. 1831 wb-5-31

Harder, William 1826 wb-4-138

Hardgraves, Samuel 1829 wb-4-447

Hardgrove, Johnson 1825 wb-4-58

Hargrove, Bennett 1843 wb-8-3

Hargrove, Bennett 1856 wb-12-288

Hargrove, Samuel 1827 wb-4-213

Harpending, Andrew 1834 wb-5-346

Harrell, James 1817 wb-2-286

Harris, Andrew 1812 wb-1-326

Harris, Carey A. 1842 wb-7-575

Harris, Carey A. 1842 wb-7-583

Harris, Henry 1821 Wb-3-213

Harris, Henry 1821 Wb-3-230

Harris, James R. 1848 wb-9-29

Harris, Rebecca L. 1851 wb-10-32

Harrison, Charles C. 1858 wb-12-533

Harrison, Jordan 1860 wb-13-196

Harrison, William P. 1842 wb-7-577

Hartley, Laban 1844 wb-8-137

Hartley, Laban 1856 wb-12-242

Hartley, Laban 1857 wb-12-332

Hasel, Elisha M. 1816 Wb-2-188

Hassell, Amelia 1825 wb-4-12

Hassell, Amillian 1825 wb-3-757

Hatcher, John B. 1857 wb-12-410

Hatcher, John R. 1857 wb-12-452

Hatcher, Octavius C. 1856 wb-12-226

Hatcher, Octavius C. 1856 wb-12-238

Hawk, Jeremiah 1842 wb-7-569

Hawkins, Amosa 1818 wb-2-392

Hawkins, Elizabeth 1858 wb-12-548

Hawkins, John 1849 wb-9-295

Hawkins, Stephen 1832 wb-5-197

Hay, Balaam 1832 wb-5-157

Hay, Balaam 1836 wb-6-156

Hay, Edith 1807 wb-1-172

Hay, James 1844 wb-8-152

Hay, John 1827 wb-4-234

Hay, John 1856 wb-12-259

Hay, Lucy 1857 wb-12-423

Hay, Martha 1843 wb-8-69

Hay, Richard 1859 wb-13-76

Hay, William 1841 wb-7-397

Hay, William H. 1849 wb-9-307

Hayes, Jane 1839 wb-7-89

Hayes, Robert 1860 wb-13-176

Haynes, Anderson 1831 wb-5-79

Haynes, F. B. 1854 wb-11-328

Haynes, Franklin B. 1854 wb-11-395

Hays, John 1832 wb-5-119

Hays, William P. 1836 wb-6-90

Hazlewood, James 1838 wb-6-512

Heaton, Dickson 1841 wb-7-408

Heaton, Enoch 1836 wb-6-100

Heaton, Mary 1839 wb-7-184

Hedlon, Enoch 1835 wb-6-69

Helm, Susanna 1854 wb-11-98

Henderson, Daniel 1825 wb-4-57

Henderson, Hugh 1815 wb-2-293

Henderson, John 1804 Wb-1-132

Henderson, Lucy 1843 wb-8-85

Henderson, Robert 1834 wb-5-426

Henderson, Robert 1836 wb-6-122

Henderson, Samuel 1829 wb-4-367

Henderson, William L. 1847 wb-8-548

Hendrix, Adam 1836 wb-6-277

Hendrix, Joseph 1855 wb-11-510

Hendrix, Thomas 1819 wb-3-100

Henry, William 1851 wb-9-661

Herbert, John B. 1848 wb-9-68

Herbert, Richard 1834 wb-5-422

Herron, Susan G. C. 1847 wb-8-540

Herron, Thomas 1823 wb-3-664

Hicks, Elijah 1844 wb-8-206

Hide, Hartwell B. 1838 wb-6-478

Higgins, Aaron D. 1853 wb-10-549

Higgins, Aaron D. 1853 wb-11-10

Higgins, John 1809 wb-1-51

Higgins, Noah 1830 wb-4-521

Higgins, Noah 1845 wb-8-260

Higgins, William 1812 wb-1-274

Hightower, Delia S. 1846 wb-8-368

Hightower, John 1802 wb-1-7

Hightower, John 1833 wb-5-339

Hightower, Joseph B. 1837 wb-6-341

Hightower, Nancy L. 1849 wb-9-302

Hightower, Richard 1821 Wb-3-254

Hightower, William 1845 wb-8-336

Hill, Benjamin 1827 wb-4-170

Hill, Dan 1826 wb-4-116

Hill, David 1843 wb-8-111

Hill, Green 1826 wb-4-66

Hill, James C. 1831 wb-5-79

Hill, James G. 1841 wb-7-476

Hill, James L. 1834 wb-5-344

Hill, John D. 1818 wb-2-410

Hill, John D. 1845 wb-8-268

Hill, John L. 1856 wb-12-215

Hill, Joshua C. 1827 wb-4-226

Hill, Joshua C. 1839 wb-7-54

Hill, Lemiza 1860 wb-13-169

Hill, Martha 1845 wb-8-293

Hill, Mary James 1838 wb-7-5

Hill, Nancy 1832 wb-5-152

Hill, Robert 1850 wb-9-430

Hill, Robert F. 1859 wb-13-121

Hill, Sarah B. 1857 wb-12-299

Hill, Spencer 1816 wb-2-213

Hill, Thomas J. 1855 wb-12-34

Hill, William 1842 wb-7-497

Hill, William C. 1812 wb-1-300

Hill, William H. 1853 wb-10-611

Hill, William H. sr. 1853 wb-11-248

Hilliard, Isaac 1832 wb-5-185

Hilliard, Mary 1848 wb-9-160

Hilliard, William H. 1833 wb-5-240

Hilton, John 1851 wb-10-2

Hilton, John B. 1853 wb-11-20

Hines, Sarah C. 1860 wb-13-196

Hinson, Tilmon D. 1861 wb-13-493

Hobbs, Hartwell 1844 wb-8-154

Hobbs, Hartwell H. 1844 wb-8-203

Hobbs, Richard 1854 wb-11-394

HoBier, Christopher A. 1841 wb-7-408

Hodge, John 1814 Wb-2-56

Hodge, John W. 1855 wb-12-1

Hodge, Louisa 1854 wb-11-327

Hodge, Robert 1853 wb-10-414

Hodges, Henry 1837 wb-6-327

Hodges, James 1829 wb-4-438

Hodges, Welcom 1807 wb-1-22

Hogan, James 1851 wb-10-116

Hogan, Sarah 1846 wb-8-491

Holland, Gustavus A. 1852 wb-10-387

Holland, John A. 1845 wb-8-346

Holland, Kemp 1825 wb-3-758

Holland, Margaret 1842 wb-7-584

Hollier, Christopher 1841 wb-7-373

Holmes, William 1851 wb-10-614

Holstead, Elisabeth 1814 Wb-2-95

Holt, Harden P. 1816 wb-2-277

Holt, John 1842 wb-7-497

Holt, Nicholas P. 1840 wb-7-329

Hood, Edward 1840 wb-7-271

Hood, John 1817 wb-2-279

Hood, Johnson 1845 wb-8-349

Hope, Thomas 1811 wb-1-239

Hopkins, James 1800 wb-1-1

Hopkins, William D. 1835 wb-6-18

Horton, Clabon 1847 wb-9-13

Horton, Claiban 1837 wb-6-325

Horton, Elizabeth 1826 wb-4-99

Horton, James D. 1852 wb-10-231

Horton, John D. 1849 wb-9-317

Hosford, Matthew 1837 wb-6-331

House, Elizabeth 1858 wb-12-509

House, Elizabeth M. 1860 wb-13-194

House, George A. 1847 wb-8-597

House, Green 1813 wb-1-333

House, Isaac 1851 wb-9-647

House, Isaac 1858 wb-12-556

House, Isaac H. 1851 wb-9-646

House, James 1825 wb-4-28

House, John 1832 wb-5-188

House, John 1836 wb-6-151

House, Joshua B. 1853 wb-10-494

House, Mansfield 1835 wb-6-73

House, William M. 1848 wb-9-171

Houston, Samuel 1809 wb-1-196

Hubbard, Woodson 1856 wb-12-218

Hudlow, George 1812 wb-1-285

Hudson, John 1830 wb-4-481

Hugely, Henry A. 1851 wb-10-30

Hughes, Albert G. 1843 wb-8-9

Hughes, Archilus 1854 wb-11-246

Hughes, George R. 1833 wb-5-337

Hughes, George W. 1838 wb-7-1

Hughes, James 1841 wb-7-459

Hughes, James 1858 wb-12-594

Hughes, John 1860 wb-13-380

Hughes, Nicholas 1840 wb-7-327

Hughes, Richard 1827 wb-4-209

Hughes, William E. 1852 wb-10-204

Hughs, Polly 1826 wb-4-75

Hulme, George W. 1834 wb-5-400

Hulme, George W. 1836 wb-6-119

Hulme, John C. 1818 wb-2-376

Hulme, Mary E. 1853 wb-10-461

Hulme, Robert 1844 wb-8-173

Hulme, Robert 1858 wb-12-553

Hulme, William 1817 wb-2-265

Humphreys, Benjamin 1815 Wb-2-161

Humphreys, Charles L. 1823 wb-3-610

Humphries, Solomon 1817 wb-2-312

Hunnell, William 1809 Wb-1-57

Hunt, Gershom 1839 wb-7-29

Hunt, Green W. 1844 wb-8-192

Hunt, Sarah 1849 wb-9-313

Hunt, Sion 1827 wb-4-177

Hunt, William C. 1860 wb-13-286

Hunter, Catharine 1831 wb-5-43

Hunter, Elijah 1817 wb-2-309

Hunter, Elisha 1829 wb-4-386

Hunter, Elizabeth 1829 wb-4-392

Hunter, James A. 1844 wb-8-147

Hunter, Joseph 1854 wb-11-307

Hutton, John M. 1833 wb-5-320

Hyde, Hartwell 1833 wb-5-291

Hyde, Richard W. 1836 wb-6-200

Ingram, Henry 1818 wb-2-379

Ingram, John 1807 wb-1-152

Ingram, Merritt 1859 wb-13-152

Ingram, Merritt 1859 wb-13-154

Ingram, Zaney 1860 wb-13-311

Inman, John 1859 wb-13-86

Iron, Fredrick W. 1816 Wb-2-188

Iron, Sarah 1815 wb-2-151

Irons, Philip Jacob 1815 wb-2-150

Irvin, Christopher 1823 wb-3-629

Irwin, David 1824 wb-3-723

Irwin, Robert 1823 wb-3-614

Ivey, David 1848 wb-9-151

Ivey, Frederick 1856 wb-12-74

Ivy, Louisa D. 1849 wb-9-301

Jackson, Duron K. 1861 wb-13-482

Jackson, Francis 1839 wb-7-26

Jackson, James 1816 wb-2-307

Jackson, Martha 1839 wb-7-169

Jackson, Mary Jane 1856 wb-12-222

Jackson, Wesley 1854 wb-11-366

Jackson, William 1817 wb-2-340

Jackson, William 1853 wb-10-493

James, George H. 1815 Wb-2-128

James, John 1839 wb-7-73

Jamison, John 1824 wb-3-741

Jamison, John B. 1860 wb-13-195

Jarrett, Amelia A. 1859 wb-13-206

Jenkins, Duke 1855 wb-12-10

Jenkins, Green 1841 wb-7-424

Jenkins, Jeremiah 1845 wb-8-252

Jennings, Lewis T. S. 1837 wb-6-355

Jennings, Lewis T. S. 1843 wb-8-121

Johnson, Allen 1836 wb-6-117

Johnson, Benjamin 1858 wb-12-535

Johnson, Charles 1815 Wb-2-162

Johnson, Gideon 1844 wb-8-142

Johnson, James 1809 wb-1-199

Johnson, James 1824 wb-3-697

Johnson, Joshua 1857 wb-12-300

Johnson, Josiah 1858 wb-12-583

Johnson, Swanson 1831 wb-5-73

Johnson, Waddy P. 1841 wb-7-424

Johnston, Andrew 1850 wb-9-376

Johnston, David 1829 wb-4-383

Johnston, Henrietta P. 1858 wb-12-481

Johnston, John 1816 wb-2-210

Johnston, Robert 1827 wb-4-205

Johnston, Stephen 1819 wb-3-42

Johnston, William 1845 wb-8-345

Jones, Benjamin 1848 wb-9-33

Jones, David G. 1835 wb-6-75

Jones, Jacob D. 1855 wb-12-24

Jones, James 1827 wb-4-220

Jones, John B. 1859 wb-13-74

Jones, Judith 1857 wb-12-363

Jones, Kiziah 1846 wb-8-489

Jones, Nancy 1827 wb-4-248

Jones, Rodham 1826 wb-4-102

Jones, Sarah 1837 wb-6-432

Jones, Taylor 1858 wb-12-551

Jones, Thomas H. 1840 wb-7-327

Jones, Wiley 1827 wb-4-175

Jones, William 1838 wb-7-5

Jones, Willie 1827 wb-4-170

Jordan, Archer 1835 wb-6-66

Jordan, Henry 1823 wb-3-653

Jordan, John 1804 Wb-1-120

Jordan, Sally 1844 wb-8-138

Jordan, Stephen 1850 wb-9-356

Jordan, Thomas 1855 wb-11-557

Jordan, William 1822 wb-3-583

Kavanaugh, Charles 1818 wb-2-376

Kearney, Lucy Davis 1815 Wb-2-135

Kellow, Thomas 1834 wb-5-400

Kennard, Hannah 1825 wb-4-4

Kennedy, Patrick 1841 wb-7-363

Kennedy, William 1853 wb-11-83

Kenny, James 1816 wb-2-194

Keyes, James A. 1860 wb-13-271

Kidd, Benjamin 1832 wb-5-200

King, Benjamin 1822 wb-3-566

King, Edward H.. 1858 wb-12-552

King, Elizabeth 1851 wb-10-42

King, Lucinda 1844 wb-8-164

King, Mary 1852 wb-10-422

King, William H. 1844 wb-8-166

Kinnard, C. W. 1856 wb-12-249

Kinnard, Christopher W. 1854 wb-11-247

Kinnard, Gabriel H. 1859 wb-13-180

Kinnard, George 1845 wb-8-342

Kinnard, George C. 1858 wb-13-14

Kinnard, Michael 1810 wb-1-222

Kinnard, Michael 1847 wb-9-18

Kinnard, Michael 1851 wb-9-695

Kirby, Malakiah 1838 wb-6-492

Kirkpatrick, Henry 1845 wb-8-336

Kirkpatrick, Henry A. 1851 wb-10-46

Kirkpatrick, John 0. 1847 wb-8-594

Lacey, Scelton 1832 wb-5-119

Ladd, William H. 1846 wb-8-447

Ladd, William H. 1846 wb-8-455

Lagron, John A. 1817 wb-2-311

Lamaster, John 1840 wb-7-347

Lamb, Alexander S. 1840 wb-7-306

Lamb, Davis 1861 wb-13-467

Lamb, Thomas 1821 Wb-3-249

Lamb, William 1848 wb-9-177

Lancaster, John 1840 wb-7-346

Landrum, Benjamin 1839 wb-7-91

Landrum, Mary 1843 wb-8-88

Landrum, Merriman 1826 wb-4-138

Lanier, Nicholas 1839 wb-7-92

Lapsley, Thomas 1831 wb-5-23

Lavender, Anthony 1854 wb-11-259

Lavender, George 1846 wb-8-476

Lavender, Nancy 1848 wb-9-64

Lawrence, Edmund 1860 wb-13-178

Layne, John 1838 wb-6-461

Layne, Thomas 1859 wb-13-87

Layne, William 1833 wb-5-272

Layne, William K. 1851 wb-10-7

Leath, Richard 1848 wb-9-146

Leaton, Hugh 1853 wb-11-52

Leaton, Reuben 1853 wb-11-51

Leaton, Susan 1845 wb-8-338

Leaton, William 1840 wb-7-221

Lee, Benjamin 1802 wb-1-9

Leigh, Benjamin 1831 wb-5-18

Leigh, Martha 1844 wb-8-154

Lemaster, Joseph 1827 wb-4-185

Lester, Barnet 1836 wb-6-260

Lester, Henry 1826 wb-4-71

Lester, Henry 1851 wb-10-160

Lester, Rebecca 1857 wb-12-306

Lester, Robert 1852 wb-10-200

Lester, Robert H. 1853 wb-10-532

Lewis, David 1814 Wb-2-97

Lewis, Elam H. 1841 wb-7-440

Lewis, Gravil 1833 wb-5-335

Lewis, Mary C. B. 1850 wb-9-381

Lightfoot, Taply M. 1849 wb-9-225

Linsey, Moses 1851 wb-9-715

Liscomb, John 1840 wb-7-270

Little, Isaac N. 1837 wb-6-316

Littleton, John 1818 wb-2-389

Mathews, Cornelius 1849 wb-9-247

Matthews, John 1851 wb-10-118

Maury, Abram 1825 wb-4-6

Maury, Abram P. 1848 wb-9-161

Maury, Elizabeth J. 1853 wb-10-487

Maury, Josephine 1852 wb-10-192

Lloyd, Lewis 1836 wb-6-235

Maury, Mary E. T. 1852 wb-10-396

Lock, Richard S. 1816 wb-2-217

Maury, Octavia 1852 wb-10-192

Locke, Green W. 1854 wb-11-373

Maury, Philip 1840 wb-7-344

Loftin, Augustine 1851 wb-9-646

Maury, Richard L. 1839 wb-7-66

Logan, Catharine 1827 wb-4-181

Maury, Thomas T. 1817 wb-2-329

Logan, William 1823 wb-3-659

Maury, Thomas T. 1837 wb-6-332

Long, Michael 1832 wb-5-181

Mayberry, Job 1845 wb-8-210

Love, Susan 1807 wb-1-29

Mayfield, George 1848 wb-9-119

Love, William 1809 Wb-1-56

Mayfield, James 1807 wb-3-66

Lowrance, John 1808 wb-1-41

Mayfield, James 1808 wb-1-199

Loyd, Lewis 1826 wb-4-96

Mayfield, John 1851 wb-10-115

Lytle, Archibald 1855 wb-11-431

Mays, Frances 1840 wb-7-303

Lytle, Elizabeth 1858 wb-12-590

Mays, Smith 1831 wb-5-77

Lytle, Elizabeth C. 1856 wb-12-284

McAlister, Charles 1825 wb-4-44

Mabane, George 1818 wb-2-407

McAlister, John 1827 wb-4-231

Mairs, Samuel 1815 Wb-2-147

McBride, Joseph 1841 wb-7-441

Mallory, James H. 1857 wb-12-355

McCabe, Charles 1828 wb-4-306

Mallory, James W. 1859 wb-13-336

McCalister, Charles 1818 wb-2-407

Mallory, John 1860 wb-13-267

McCall, Francis 1808 wb-1-201

Mallory, Roger 1838 wb-6-477

McCaul, James 1853 wb-10-588

Mallory, Thomas G. 1832 wb-5-161

McClaran, Alexander 1816 wb-2-275

Mangrum, Pleasant 1858 wb-12-486

McClaran, Clem 1849 wb-9-291

Manire, John 1809 wb-1-323

McClaran, Thomas 1827 wb-4-252

Manire, Lemuel 1837 wb-6-339

McClellan, Sarah E. 1859 wb-13-70

Manley, Caleb 1831 wb-5-69

McClure, Henry 1855 wb-11-578

Manley, Richard 1847 wb-9-5

McCollum, Elizabeth 1852 wb-10-392

Manly, John 1855 wb-11-563

McCollum, John 1842 wb-7-577

Manson, Nancy W. 1857 wb-12-328

McCombs, Elizabeth 1844 wb-8-136

Manson, Susan A. C. 1848 wb-9-58

McConnico, Frances W. 1848 wb-9-36

Marable, Silas 1850 wb-9-470

McConnico, Garner 1835 wb-6-47

Marks, William 1838 wb-6-450

McConnico, Jared 1803 Wb-1-102

Marling, George 1854 wb-11-310

McConnico, Jared 1816 wb-2-221

Marr, Nicholas L. 1858 wb-12-528

McConnico, Jared 1834 wb-5-346

Marshall, Ann 1861 wb-13-407

McConnico, Keziah 1818 wb-2-377

Marshall, Ann 1861 wb-13-408

McConnico, Mary 1839 wb-7-72

Marshall, Elizabeth 1854 wb-11-88

McCord, Abner 1832 wb-5-163

Marshall, Elizabeth 1855 wb-11-500

McCord, David 1819 wb-3-80

Marshall, Gilbert 1857 wb-12-414

McCord, David 1834 wb-5-363

Marshall, W. S. 1857 wb-12-375

McCord, Elizabeth 1834 wb-5-361

Marshall, William 1826 wb-4-92

McCord, George 1857 wb-12-400

Marshall, William S. 1857 wb-12-376

McCord, Harvey B. 1838 wb-6-448

Martin, Alexander 1812 wb-3-79

McCord, Henry B. 1836 wb-6-114

Martin, Daniel 1859 wb-13-55

McCord, James 1851 wb-10-63

Martin, Daniel G. 1859 wb-13-56

McCord, John 1826 wb-4-99

Martin, Hudson 1859 wb-13-26

McCoy, William 1836 wb-6-242

Martin, Scipio 1829 wb-4-374

McCoy, William 1849 wb-9-242

Martin, William 1843 wb-8-127

McCrady, Andrew 1839 wb-7-129

Martin, William H. 1858 wb-13-13

McCrory, John 1858 wb-12-567

Mason, Henriana 1848 wb-9-38

McCrory, Thomas 1819 wb-3-97

Massey, Mary J. 1858 wb-12-528

McCurdy, David 1834 wb-5-423

McCutchen, Benjamin 1851 wb-9-669

McPherson, Cornelius 1838 wb-7-18

McCutchen, Catharine 1857 wb-12-365

McPherson, Jonathan 1815 Wb-2-168

McCutchen, Catharine E. 1846 wb-8-499

McSwine, John 1815 wb-2-150

McCutchen, James 1810 wb-1-237

Meacham, Green 1852 wb-10-423

McCutchen, Mary M. 1844 wb-8-197

Meacham, James 1851 wb-10-35

McCutchen, Patrick 1812 wb-1-307

Meador, Joseph 1832 wb-5-156

McCutchen, Patrick 1841 wb-7-377

Meador, Joseph R. 1848 wb-9-34

McCutchen, Samuel 1816 wb-2-243

Meador, William 1840 wb-7-297

McEwen, Cyrus J. 1853 wb-10-463

Meadow, William 1837 wb-6-362

McEwen, David 1822 wb-3-294

Meadows, Anderson 1827 wb-4-215

McEwen, Felix G. 1831 wb-5-56

Medley, Francis 1829 wb-4-443

McEwen, James 1822 wb-3-296

Melton, Susan 1850 wb-9-584

McEwen, James 1828 wb-4-280

Merritt, Ann D. 1854 wb-11-268

McEwen, Sarah 1851 wb-10-65

Merritt, James 1837 wb-6-353

McEwen, William 1816 wb-2-216

Merritt, James 1837 wb-6-417

McFadden, James 1815 wb-2-153

Merritt, John A. 1853 wb-11-47

McFadden, Mary Jane 1848 wb-9-148

Merritt, Shimmey 1856 wb-12-208

McFadden, Robert 1823 wb-3-640

Merritt, Thomas 1857 wb-12-424

McFaddin, Candour 1832 wb-5-140

Miller, Thomas 1822 wb-3-300

McFarland, Charles 1861 wb-13-475

Mills, Sharod 1815 Wb-2-128

McFarland, John 1853 wb-11-1

Mills, Sharod 1815 Wb-2-129

McFarlen, Charles J. 1861 wb-13-421

Mincy, Philip 1857 wb-12-463

McGan, Eli 1855 wb-11-564

Mincy, Susan 1858 wb-12-545

McGavock, Lucinda 1848 wb-9-121

Mitchell, Evan 1810 wb-1-215

McGavock, Lysander 1855 wb-11-579

Mitchell, Vachel 1855 wb-12-24

McGavock, Randal 1843 wb-8-108

Montgomery, Alexander 1830 wb-4-496

McGee, Anthony W. 1854 wb-11-93

Montgomery, Cyrus 1854 wb-11-377

McGee, William 1832 wb-5-183

Montgomery, Hannah 1806 wb-1-21

McGilvray, William 1831 wb-5-22

Montgomery, John 1818 wb-2-395

McHughs, Moses 1804 wb-1-133

Montgomery, Moses 1817 wb-2-286

McKay, James M. 1836 wb-6-259

Montgomery, Robert 1830 wb-4-538

McKay, Mary 1846 wb-8-481

Montgomery, Silas 1854 wb-11-375

McKay, Milton R. 1839 wb-7-29

Moore, Alfred 1837 wb-6-299

McKay, William 1836 wb-6-117

Moore, Benjamin 1849 wb-9-273

McKinney, Ebenezer 1816 wb-2-239

Moore, Carey H. 1834 wb-5-421

McKinney, John 1816 wb-2-226

Moore, Catharine 1806 wb-1-156

McKinney, John 1840 wb-7-313

Moore, Ferdinand 1840 wb-7-359

McKinney, Randolph 1827 wb-4-269

Moore, James 1805 Wb-1-121

McKnight, William 1806 wb-1-148

Moore, James 1838 wb-6-525

McLain, Dorcas 1840 wb-7-220

Moore, James jr. 1815 Wb-2-137

McLain, Jane 1841 wb-7-426

Moore, Jane W. 1847 wb-8-599

McLemore, Atkins J. 1849 wb-9-303

Moore, John W. 1853 wb-11-52

McLemore, Bethenia S. 1857 wb-12-429

Moore, Moses 1817 wb-2-204

McLemore, Robert 1823 wb-3-625

Moran, John 1846 wb-8-449

McLemore, Robert 1836 wb-6-119

Morris, Ann E. 1859 wb-13-116

McLemore, Sidney Smith 1860 wb-13-197

Morris, Mathew E. 1853 wb-10-466

McLemore, Young 1804 wb-1-10

Morris, Nathan 1849 wb-9-252

McLemore, Young 1823 wb-3-661

Morris, Nathan E. 1849 wb-9-266

McLemore, Young 1824 wb-3-749

Morris, William 1822 wb-3-570

McMahan, Daniel 1838 wb-7-3

Morrison, Mary 1817 wb-2-340

McMoss, Abram 1836 wb-6-118

Morton, Abner W. 1830 wb-4-479

McMullen, Andrew 1802 Wb-1-101

Morton, Abraham B. 1854 wb-11-320

McMurray, John 1852 wb-10-429

Morton, Cynthia 1855 wb-11-488

McNeil, Lemuel S. 1827 wb-4-174

Morton, Elisha 1821 wb-3-281

McPhail, Daniel 1846 wb-8-492

Morton, Jacob sr. 1854 wb-11-368

McPhail, Sarah 1851 wb-10-48

Morton, Leevicy 1833 wb-5-340

Morton, Penisa 1853 wb-11-29

Morton, Samuel 1825 wb-4-52

Morton, Samuel 1836 wb-6-187

Morton, Samuel 1851 wb-9-665

Morton, Seth 1836 wb-6-280

Morton, Step 1838 wb-7-13

Morton, Susan 1854 wb-11-401

Morton, Thomas 1815 wb-2-148

Morton, William 1822 wb-3-584

Morton, William B. 1859 wb-13-88

Morton, William C. 1837 wb-6-368

Morton, William E. 1850 wb-9-655

Moses, Abram R. 1822 wb-3-302

Moss, Henry 1857 wb-12-358

Motheral, Jane 1833 wb-5-310

Motheral, John 1824 wb-3-724

Moulton, Thomas 1822 wb-3-577

Mullen, Jesse 1828 wb-4-352

Mullen, Jesse 1829 wb-4-373

Mullin, Henry 1847 wb-9-8

Mullin, William S. 1806 wb-1-192

Murfree, Hardy 1809 Wb-1-87

Murfree, Hardy 1818 wb-2-458

Murfree, William H. 1827 wb-4-208

Murphrey, Laurence 1816 wb-2-274

Newsom, John R. 1852 wb-10-375

Newsom, Lawrence 1816 wb-2-255

Newsom, Mary 1838 wb-6-539

Newsom, Nathaniel 1831 wb-5-9

Nichols, Allen 1848 wb-9-143

Nichols, Allen F. 1851 wb-10-4

Nichols, Ferdinando S. 1859 wb-13-145

Nicholson, Mala 1829 wb-4-435

Nicholson, Malachi 1829 wb-4-463

Nicholson, Malachi 1849 wb-9-233

Nicholson, Marmaduke N. 1836 wb-6-21

Nicholson, Sarah 1848 wb-9-161

Noland, John 1807 wb-1-170

Nolen, Berry 1850 wb-9-592

Nolen, David 1839 wb-7-203

Nolen, David 1851 wb-10-123

Nolen, General L. 1851 wb-10-135

Nolen, General L. 1851 wb-10-322

Nolen, General Lee 1860 wb-13-349

Nolen, John 1857 wb-12-368

Nolen, Mary a. 1860 wb-13-353

Nolen, Stephen 1851 wb-10-51

Nolen, Thomas J. 1853 wb-10-488

Nolen, William 1842 wb-7-575

Nolen, William 1850 wb-9-407

Murrell, Jeffery 1825 wb-3-755

Nolen, William M. W. 1861 wb-13-404

Murrey, William 1803 Wb-1-111

Norris, James 1815 Wb-2-137

Murry, Riley D. 1861 wb-13-472

North, Abram 1840 wb-7-318

Murry, Robert 1815 Wb-2-147

North, Abram 1856 wb-12-69

Nall, William 1843 wb-8-15

North, Elisha 1837 wb-6-383

Nash, Charles 1826 wb-4-111

North, James 1836 wb-6-258

Nash, Dempsey 1833 wb-5-278

North, James H. 1855 wb-11-455

Neal, James J. 1849 wb-9-333

North, John 1836 wb-6-233

Neal, William 1833 wb-5-274

North, John E. F. 1843 wb-8-62

Neeley, Elijah L. 1846 wb-8-451

North, William T. 1848 wb-9-60

Neely, George 1817 wb-2-353

North, William T. 1854 wb-11-91

Neelly, James 1819 wb-3-40

Norton, William 1813 wb-2-30

Neelly, James 1835 wb-6-68

Norton, William 1830 wb-4-501

Neelly, Jane 1842 wb-7-543

Nowlen, John 1811 wb-1-260

Neelly, John 1818 wb-2-411

Nunn, Francis 1816 Wb-2-182

Neelly, Robert 1815 wb-2-153

Nunn, Francis 1841 wb-7-368

Neelly, Sophia 1831 wb-5-29

O'Donnel, Matthew 1823 wb-3-609

Neely, Charles 1822 wb-3-566

Oakes, Isaac 1824 wb-3-673

Neely, George 1833 wb-5-309

Oden, Solomon 1860 wb-13-273

Neely, George 1836 wb-6-130

Odil, James M. 1842 wb-7-555

Neely, George L. 1860 wb-13-223

Ogilvie, Cynthia M. 1854 wb-11-89

Neely, James 1834 wb-5-351

Ogilvie, Jason W. 1848 wb-9-134

Neely, James 1836 wb-6-120

Ogilvie, John 1822 wb-3-291

Neely, William 1827 wb-4-203

Ogilvie, Richard 1822 wb-3-588

Neilly, Charles S. 1822 wb-3-598

Ogilvie, William 1813 wb-1-313

Nelson, C. H. 1849 wb-9-253

Old, Thomas 1831 wb-5-23

Nevills, Christiana T. 1859 wb-13-186

Oldham, Bishop 1841 wb-7-380

Nevils, Ann E. 1855 wb-11-577

Oldham, Elizabeth 1841 wb-7-380

Nevils, Josiah 1854 wb-11-403

Oram, Eliza P. 1841 wb-7-411

Newsom, Benjamin L. 1849 wb-9-226

Oram, William H. 1841 wb-7-396

Newsom, James 1838 wb-6-493

Orman, Joseph 1857 wb-12-385

Ormond, Adam 1851 wb-10-54

Orms, Evan B. 1856 wb-12-75

Orr, William 1822 wb-3-330

Ortin, Jane 1823 wb-3-610

Orton, Richard 1824 wb-3-720

Parrish, Joel 1812 wb-1-272

Parrish, Matthew F. 1845 wb-8-296

Parrish, Robert 1827 wb-4-254

Parrish, Robert E. 1845 wb-8-296

Parrish, Sarah P. 1845 wb-8-296

Orton, William 1803 wb-1-138

Parrish, Susanna 1845 wb-8-264

Orum, James 1853 wb-10-587

Parsley, Drury W. 1848 wb-9-211

Osburn, Nancy 1851 wb-10-37

Parsley, John 1844 wb-8-197

Oslin, William 1826 wb-4-101

Pate, Rosannah 1861 wb-13-419

Owen, Eliza A. 1857 wb-12-470

Pate, Thomas Sr. 1833 wb-5-266

Owen, Everett 1859 wb-13-208

Patillo, David 1861 wb-13-494

Owen, Jabez 1850 wb-9-431

Patterson, William 1816 wb-2-202

Owen, James 1831 wb-5-72

Patton, Andrew J. 1854 wb-11-306

Owen, James S. 1852 wb-10-197

Patton, James 1807 wb-1-150

Owen, Nathaniel R. 1846 wb-8-484

Patton, James 1819 wb-3-108

Owen, Philip 1854 wb-11-177

Patton, James 1832 wb-5-199

Owen, Richard A. 1852 wb-10-390

Patton, James 1833 wb-5-221

Owen, Richard C. 1860 wb-13-225

Patton, Jason 1841 wb-7-478

Owen, Robert 1841 wb-7-361

Patton, John 1809 wb-1-203

Owen, Samuel 1839 wb-7-34

Patton, John 1819 wb-3-31

Owen, Samuel 1840 wb-7-272

Patton, Robert 1834 wb-5-395

Owen, Sandy G. 1858 wb-13-6

Patton, Robert 1844 wb-8-203

Owen, William 1852 wb-10-425

Patton, Sarah 1852 wb-10-205

Owens, William 1815 wb-2-149

Patton, Sarah F. 1852 wb-10-256

Owings, Elijah 1804 wb-1-13

Patton, Thomas W. 1848 wb-9-38

Ozburn, James 1848 wb-9-27

Patton, Tristram 1855 wb-11-580

Ozburn, Jane 1850 wb-9-422

Patton, William 1846 wb-8-448

Ozburn, Robert 1852 wb-10-390

Patton, William 1847 wb-8-607

Ozburne, Richie 1848 wb-9-149

Payne, William 1831 wb-5-2

Padgett, Henry G. 1853 wb-11-45

Peach, John 1859 wb-13-73

Padgett, Mary 1856 wb-12-49

Peach, John 1859 wb-13-83

Page, David D. 1817 wb-2-364

Pearcy, Algernon 1834 wb-5-390

Page, David D. 1824 wb-3-672

Pearcy, Algernon 1836 wb-6-182

Page, John 1808 wb-1-185

Pearre, James 1841 wb-7-403

Palmore, Thomas 1860 wb-13-266

Pearre, Joshua 1847 wb-9-20

Parham, Elizabeth 1855 wb-12-26

Pearre, Joshua W. 1839 wb-7-145

Parham, George 1850 wb-9-342

Pearre, Milly Ann 1853 wb-11-81

Parham, Rebecca 1818 wb-2-362

Pearre, William W. 1850 wb-9-341

Parham, Thomas 1832 wb-5-196

Peay, Mary 1822 wb-3-314

Park, Martha J. 1849 wb-9-277

Peay, Samuel 1854 wb-11-318

Park, Rhoda 1852 wb-10-387

Peay, Susannah 1857 wb-12-327

Parker, George 1816 wb-2-274

Peay, Thomas 1837 wb-6-416

Parker, George W. 1844 wb-8-150

Peay, Thomas 1838 wb-6-471

Parker, John 1851 wb-9-682

Peay, Thomas Sr. 1858 wb-12-547

Parks, John 1823 wb-3-608

Peebles, Alexander 1831 wb-5-86

Parks, John 1836 wb-6-151

Pennington, Clement S. 1854 wb-11-264

Parks, John 1850 wb-9-429

Perkins, Daniel 1834 wb-5-424

Parks, Rachael 1834 wb-5-403

Perkins, Daniel 1845 wb-8-325

Parks, Stephen N. 1858 wb-12-501

Perkins, John P. 1807 wb-1-162

Parks, William 1815 wb-2-152

Perkins, John P. 1820 wb-3-210

Parmely, Giles 1803 wb-1-8

Perkins, Mary 1833 wb-5-318

Parrett, Caleb 1843 wb-8-59

Perkins, Nicholas 1848 wb-9-93

Parrish, Abram M. 1828 wb-4-300

Perkins, Nicholas T. 1843 wb-8-102

Parrish, David W. 1845 wb-8-296

Perkins, Peter (Colonel) 1813 wb-1-310

Parrish, Elijah R. 1840 wb-7-315

Perkins, Samuel 1843 wb-8-48

Parrish, James D. 1836 wb-6-258

Perkins, Samuel 1861 wb-13-409

Perkins, Thomas H. 1839 wb-7-213

Powell, Elias 1852 wb-10-400

Powell, Milton 1847 wb-8-551

Poyner, William 1830 wb-4-501

Poynor, Charles M. 1849 wb-9-277

Poynor, John 1852 wb-10-200

Poynor, Robert 1848 wb-9-144

Perkins, Thomas Hardin 1834 wb-5-359

Perry, Richardson 1816 Wb-2-189

Pettus, Elizabeth 0. 1856 wb-12-290

Pettus, Susannah 1861 wb-13-385

Pettus, Susannah 1861 wb-13-400

Petway, John S. 1833 wb-5-238

Pratt, Ann 1860 wb-13-319

Petway, Mary 1833 wb-5-237

Price, James 1844 wb-8-188

Petway, William 1826 wb-4-116

Price, Mary 1858 wb-12-578

Pewett, Catharine 1823 wb-3-630

Price, William A. 1852 wb-10-389

Pewett, James 1822 wb-3-595

Prichard, Isaac C. 1845 wb-8-229

Pewett, James 1854 wb-11-100

Prichard, Robert 1847 wb-8-532

Pewett, Joel 1823 wb-3-641

Priest, John T. 1810 wb-1-216

Pewett, Joseph 1822 wb-3-333

Priest, Nancy 1858 wb-12-569

Pewit, Joseph 1840 wb-7-328

Primm, Jeremiah 1860 wb-13-355

Pewitt, Susanna 1848 wb-9-177

Primm, John 1819 wb-3-99

Philips, Isaac M. 1839 wb-7-177

Primm, Sally 1838 wb-6-526

Philips, Jessee H. 1852 wb-10-399

Prior, Luke 1848 wb-9-172

Philips, Joseph 1833 wb-5-270

Pritchard, Samuel N. 1859 wb-13-52

Phillips, William 1819 wb-3-4

Pritchett, Robert 1849 wb-9-327

Phipps, Jordan 1827 wb-4-234

Pritchett, Thomas J. 1848 wb-9-45

Phipps, Montgomery B. 1852 wb-10-401

Prowell, Thomas 1840 wb-7-304

Phipps, Robert W. 1844 wb-8-214

Prowell, Thomas 1855 wb-11-505

Pickard, George M. 1836 wb-6-232

Prowell, Thomas 1855 wb-11-559

Pigg, Stephen 1827 wb-4-256

Pryor, Eleanor 1851 wb-10-9

Pinkston, David 1851 wb-9-709

Pryor, John 1810 wb-1-240

Pinkston, Francis 1860 wb-13-177

Pryor, Nelly 1849 wb-9-335

Pinkston, Peter 1840 wb-7-248

Puckett, Richard 1813 wb-2-30

Polk, John 1851 wb-10-323

Pulliam, Mary 1833 wb-5-220

Polk, Richard 1837 wb-6-343

Puryear, Hezekiah 1816 wb-2-233

Pollard, Joseph 1841 wb-7-421

Puryear, Jordan R. H. 1847 wb-8-585

Pope, Ann 1836 wb-6-278

Puryear, Matilda 1835 wb-6-77

Pope, Ann 1837 wb-6-297

Puryear, William Augustus 1849 wb-9-228

Pope, Ezekiel 1829 wb-4-368

Putman, Jabin 1836 wb-6-279

Pope, Gustavus A. 1834 wb-5-383

Putman, James 1836 wb-6-248

Pope, Isac W. 1840 wb-7-217

Putnam, Jabin 1836 wb-6-115

Pope, Jane 0. 1833 wb-5-293

Pyron, Charles 1847 wb-8-588

Pope, John 1829 wb-4-436

Quinn, Enoch 1832 wb-5-155

Pope, John 1840 wb-7-268

Quinn, Sarah 1823 wb-3-612

Pope, John W. 1842 wb-7-512

Radford, Emily S. 1854 wb-11-181

Pope, Mary C. 1838 wb-6-491

Radford, James 1815 Wb-2-165

Pope, William R. 1846 wb-8-409

Radford, John 1815 wb-2-148

Porter, Dudley 1812 wb-1-287

Radford, William 1833 wb-5-228

Porter, Jessee 1824 wb-3-674

Ragsdale, Daniel 1841 wb-7-401

Porter, John 1828 wb-4-287

Ragsdale, Daniel 1841 wb-7-403

Porter, John B. 1848 wb-9-86

Ragsdale, Edward 1823 wb-3-628

Porter, Miriam 1841 wb-7-407

Ragsdale, Edward 1836 wb-6-117

Porter, Thomas D. 1837 wb-6-384

Ragsdale, James 1850 wb-9-585

Poteet, Isaac 1837 wb-6-429

Ragsdale, Penelope 1850 wb-9-416

Poteet, John 1831 wb-5-45

Ragsdale, Thomas 1858 wb-12-568

Potter, Frances 1844 wb-8-196

Raigains, Thomas 1834 wb-5-420

Potts, Daniel 1845 wb-8-309

Ralston, Robert 1857 wb-12-474

Potts, James 1844 wb-8-207

Rankin, Samuel K. 1847 wb-8-517

Potts, Joseph 1812 wb-1-277

Ransom, Richard 1836 wb-6-115

Potts, Peter 1815 wb-2-147

Rash, Robert 1844 wb-8-173

Potts, Stephen 1852 wb-10-206

Rash, Stephen H. 1855 wb-12-13

Ratcliffe, Gideon 1854 wb-11-179

Rea, Tabitha 1855 wb-11-561

Read, Josiah 1842 wb-7-530

Read, Josiah 1842 wb-7-534

Reams, Andrew D. 1840 wb-7-333

Reams, Henry 1836 wb-6-214

Reams, Henry 1836 wb-6-248

Reams, Henry 1846 wb-8-462

Reams, Joshua 1859 wb-13-119

Reams, Nancy 1849 wb-9-285

Reams, Oscar 1861 wb-13-440

Reams, Robert 1860 wb-13-216

Reams, Robert 1860 wb-13-222

Reams, William 1841 wb-7-425

Redd, Robert S. 1841 wb-7-368

Redford, Sally 1818 wb-2-410

Redford, William 1832 wb-5-202

Redmond, James 1849 wb-9-252

Reed, Alexander 1825 wb-4-66

Reed, Andrew 1836 wb-6-199

Reed, Edward 1816 Wb-2-191

Reese, Jordon 1813 wb-1-315

Reese, Sarah 1824 wb-3-698

Reeves, Peter 1812 wb-1-288

Reeves, Peter 1822 wb-3-579

Region, Joel 1842 wb-7-541

Reid, Alexander 1816 wb-2-207

Reid, John 1816 wb-2-209

Reid, John 1827 wb-4-171

Revel, Kinchen 1829 wb-4-371

Reynolds, George 1813 Wb-2-38

Reynolds, John G. 1858 wb-12-503

Reynolds, Mary W. 1846 wb-8-456

Reynolds, Prepare 1832 wb-5-203

Reynolds, Richard 1836 wb-6-168

Reynolds, Richard C. 1826 wb-4-94

Reynolds, Spencer 1830 wb-4-517

Reynolds, Spencer 1844 wb-8-176

Reynolds, Spencer 1845 wb-8-244

Reynolds, Spencer 1856 wb-12-95

Reynolds, Susanna 1821 Wb-3-274

Reynolds, Thomas 1839 wb-7-173

Reynolds, Thomas P. 1847 wb-8-517

Rice, Francis 1860 wb-13-333

Rice, Isham 1855 wb-12-27

Rice, James 1835 wb-6-56

Rice, James 1847 wb-8-540

Richardson, Conrad 1857 wb-12-369

Richardson, John 1860 wb-13-164

Richardson, Robert G. 1861 wb-13-420

Ridley, Beverly 1845 wb-8-246

Ridley, Beverly 1845 wb-8-314

Ridley, George G. 1845 wb-8-328

Ridley, William 1852 wb-10-220

Ridley, William B. 1852 wb-10-193

Riggs, Wright 1812 wb-1-330

Riggs, Zadock 1816 wb-2-232

Ripley, Eliza 1841 wb-7-407

Rivers, Ephraim 1851 wb-10-1

Rivers, James J. 1841 wb-7-363

Rivers, Robert 1848 wb-9-186

Roach, Simon 1856 wb-12-76

Robards, Sarah 1848 wb-9-167

Roberds, William 1820 wb-3-163

Roberts, Benjamin 1830 wb-4-515

Roberts, Benjamin 1846 wb-8-391

Roberts, Hannah L. 1834 wb-5-354

Roberts, Hannah S. 1836 wb-6-158

Roberts, John 1824 wb-3-677

Roberts, John 1859 wb-13-163

Roberts, Joseph 1810 wb-1-226

Roberts, Lemuel 1822 wb-3-594

Roberts, Lucy F. 1836 wb-6-218

Robertson, Charles 1829 wb-4-466

Robertson, David 1821 wb-3-275

Robertson, Edward 1829 wb-4-423

Robertson, Hardy 1835 wb-6-45

Robertson, Mary A. L. 1842 wb-7-585

Robertson, Richard 1852 wb-10-193

Robeson, R. W. 1850 wb-9-585

Robinson, Alexander M. 1847 wb-8-613

Robinson, Charles 1828 wb-4-286

Robinson, David R. 1839 wb-7-51

Robinson, James C. 1852 wb-10-416

Robinson, James S. 1856 wb-12-55

Robinson, John D. 1860 wb-13-283

Robinson, Malinda B. 1855 wb-12-32

Robinson, Michael 1808 wb-1-201

Robinson, Michael 1840 wb-7-325

Robinson, Michael 1851 wb-9-679

Robinson, Thomas L. 1850 wb-9-378

Robison, George R. 1836 wb-6-228

Robison, Richard W. 1850 wb-9-602

Rodgers, Andrew H. 1858 wb-12-508

Rogers, Charles 1825 wb-4-5

Rogers, James 1815 wb-2-149

Rogers, Robert 1819 wb-3-38

Rogers, Samuel 1816 Wb-2-183

Rogers, Thomas 1807 wb-1-177

Rolland, Jacob 1812 wb-2-10

Roper, David 1845 wb-8-337

Roper, David E. 1846 wb-8-372

Roper, Eliza 1846 wb-8-372

Roper, Eliza Ann 1848 wb-9-55

Roper, Martha B. 1846 wb-8-371

Roper, Martha P. 1848 wb-9-55

Rouden, Sally 1823 wb-3-658

Roundtree, Cicero 1850 wb-9-458

Rowlett, John 1827 wb-4-247

Rowlett, Martin 1842 wb-7-529

Rowlett, Prudence 1833 wb-5-274

Royster, Keturah 1840 wb-7-217

Rucker, Elizabeth 1845 wb-8-365

Rucker, John 1845 wb-8-342

Rucker, Sarah 1845 wb-8-326

Rucker, William 1846 wb-8-495

Rucker, William sr. 1826 wb-4-140

Rudder, Epaphroditus 1847 wb-8-535

Rudder, Manoah B. 1846 wb-8-491

Rudder, Richard H. 1853 wb-10-418

Russell, Benjamin 1845 wb-8-329

Rutledge, Robert 1819 wb-3-26

Rutledge, William 1807 wb-1-161

Rutledge, William 1809 Wb-1-55

Ryan, Richard 1839 wb-7-29

Sammons, Sally 1844 wb-8-158

Sample, James 1816 wb-2-233

Sample, John 1817 wb-2-313

Sample, William 1816 wb-2-219

Sampson, Richard 1818 wb-2-389

Sandford, Robert 1818 wb-2-409

Sanford, James 1845 wb-8-327

Sanford, Reuben 1846 wb-8-494

Sappington, Elizabeth 1840 wb-7-290

Sasser, Stephen 1827 wb-4-160

Satterfield, John 1852 wb-10-211

Sawyer, Dempsey 1860 wb-13-341

Sayers, Robert A. 1856 wb-12-53

Scales, Absalom 1832 wb-5-161

Scales, Absalom 1835 wb-6-46

Scales, Charlotte G. 1860 wb-13-300

Scales, Daniel 1836 wb-6-146

Scales, Daniel 1840 wb-7-263

Scales, Fanny 1827 wb-4-180

Scales, Joab 1848 wb-9-72

Scales, John 1859 wb-13-140

Scales, John M. 1839 wb-7-142

Scales, John M. 1839 wb-7-210

Scales, John M. 1839 wb-7-212

Scales, John M. 1840 wb-7-218

Scales, Joseph H. 1856 wb-12-273

Scales, Nancy 1838 wb-6-494

Scales, Noah 1860 wb-13-236

Scales, Robert 1860 wb-13-299

Scales, Samuel 1837 wb-6-305

Scales, William G. 1841 wb-7-397

Scales, William G. 1851 wb-9-674

Scott, James 1832 wb-5-127

Scott, Thomas 1838 wb-6-461

Scruggs, Drury 1850 wb-9-409

Scruggs, Edward 1847 wb-8-587

Scruggs, John 1851 wb-10-90

Scruggs, John B. 1845 wb-8-228

Scruggs, John H. 1855 wb-11-440

Scruggs, Keziah 1829 wb-4-381

Scruggs, William 1859 wb-13-67

Searight, George 1847 wb-8-604

Searight, Marcus 1860 wb-13-376

Seay, Elizabeth W. 1836 wb-6-225

Seay, John 1812 wb-1-276

Secrest, John 1836 wb-6-124

Secrest, John 1847 wb-9-17

Sellars, John C. 1855 wb-11-488

Sellers, John 1853 wb-10-483

Shannon, David 1821 Wb-3-261

Shannon, David 1839 wb-7-71

Shannon, George 1836 wb-6-235

Shannon, Robert Mc(Knight) W. 1828 wb-4-306

Shannon, Robert Washington 1861 wb-13-458

Sharp, Anthony 1812 wb-2-1

Sharp, Thomas 1808 wb-1-189

Shaw, Alexander 1826 wb-4-103

Shaw, Eliza 1848 wb-9-192

Shaw, Nathaniel 1857 wb-12-408

Shegog, James 1853 wb-10-408

Shelburn, James 1813 wb-2-18

Shelburn, James 1839 wb-7-205

Shelburne, Parmelia 1858 wb-12-546

Shelton, Marshall 1838 wb-6-462

Shenall, Keziah 1816 wb-2-214

Shepherd, John 1812 wb-1-306

Sheppard, James 1828 wb-4-346

Shores, John 1815 wb-2-151

Shumate, James 1813 wb-2-33

Shumate, John 1808 wb-1-179

Simmonds, Thomas H. 1856 wb-13-170

Simmons, Hardeman 1837 wb-6-296

Simmons, Hardy 1835 wb-6-52

Simmons, Thomas 1794 wb-1-244

Simons, Hardy 1837 wb-6-304

Sims, Boyd M. 1849 wb-9-290

Sims, John G. 1844 wb-8-189

Skelley, James 1816 wb-2-207

Skinner, Gilly G. 1858 wb-12-508

Slaughter, Lucy B. 1848 wb-9-59

Slaven, Alexander 1848 wb-9-30

Sledge, John 1823 wb-3-644

Sledge, John 1860 wb-13-218

Slicker, George sr. 1828 wb-4-307

Smith, Alexander 1841 wb-7-411

Smith, Andrew 1836 wb-6-200

Smith, Andrew G. 1836 wb-6-206

Smith, Antoinette 1852 wb-10-369

Smith, Edwin 1857 wb-12-471

Smith, Isaac 1850 wb-9-437

Smith, John 1825 wb-4-54

Smith, John 1856 wb-12-72

Smith, John F. 1836 wb-6-95

Smith, Laura L. 1844 wb-8-207

Smith, Lemuel 1844 wb-8-147

Smith, Luke 1809 wb-1-52

Smith, Luke L. 1853 wb-10-489

Smith, Mary A. E. 1842 wb-7-498

Smith, Nicholas P. 1833 wb-5-242

Smith, Peter N. 1836 wb-6-222

Smith, Rachel 1825 wb-3-765

Smith, Richard 1814 Wb-2-55

Smith, Samuel 1817 wb-2-310

Smith, Samuel 1850 wb-9-459

Smith, Sherwood 1851 wb-10-29

Smith, Thomas B. 1838 wb-7-6

Smith, Thomas S. 1844 wb-8-152

Smith, William 1815 Wb-2-165

Smith, William 1832 wb-5-120

Smithson, Clement 1814 Wb-2-105

Smithson, Elizabeth C. 1839 wb-7-71

Smithson, John 1837 wb-6-400

Smithson, Nathaniel B. 1859 wb-13-150

Smithson, Richard K. 1836 wb-6-216

Smithson, Samuel C. 1838 wb-6-441

Sneed, Alexander 1853 wb-10-458

Sneed, Alexander E. 1853 wb-10-532

Sneed, James 1853 wb-11-37

Sneed, Mark A. 1854 wb-11-173

Sneed, Susan 1861 wb-13-448

Southall, James 1845 wb-8-344

Sparkman, Jesse 1846 wb-8-392

Sparkman, Kinchen 1836 wb-6-213

Sparkman, Kinchen 1846 wb-8-472

Sparkman, Martha M. 1846 wb-8-463

Sparkman, William 1832 wb-5-153

Sparkman, William C. 1854 wb-11-95

Sprott, James A. 1859 wb-13-80

Squier, David 1819 wb-3-3

Squier, Gurdon 1813 Wb-2-36

Stacy, Daniel B. 1831 wb-5-4

Staggs, Felix 1826 wb-4-139

Staggs, John 1827 wb-4-156

Stancil, Elizabeth 1848 wb-9-168

Stancill, Nathan 1822 wb-3-326

Stanfield, Ephraim 1815 wb-2-159

Stanfield, Robert G. 1855 wb-11-558

Stanfield, Spivey 1842 wb-7-535

Stanley, Martin 1822 wb-3-326

Stanley, Martin 1836 wb-6-264

Stanley, Wright 1833 wb-5-296

Stanley, Wright 1836 wb-6-161

Starnes, Samuel 1850 wb-9-346

Starnes, Samuel S. 1842 wb-7-586

Starnes, Shubal 1851 wb-10-26

Starnes, Shubart? 1848 wb-9-165

Steele, Alexander 1846 wb-8-449

Steele, Moses 1844 wb-8-169

Steele, Sarah R. 1853 wb-11-3

Stephen, Martha 1858 wb-12-547

Stephens, Dennis 1858 wb-12-548

Stephens, Edward 1836 wb-6-276

Stephens, Loami 1815 Wb-2-164

Stephens, Luraney 1839 wb-7-70

Stephens, Silas 1838 wb-6-504

Stephens, Silas 1838 wb-7-25

Stephens, Thomas 1854 wb-11-402

Stephens, William sr. 1816 Wb-2-184

Stephenson, James W. 1848 wb-9-145

Stephenson, Nathaniel 1848 wb-9-38

Stephenson, Rosanna D. 1849 wb-9-289

Stevens, Edward 1837 wb-6-330

Stevens, Henry C. 1840 wb-7-277

Stevens, Henry C. 1850 wb-9-581

Stevens, James P. 1852 wb-10-266

Stevens, Joel 1847 wb-9-2

Stevenson, James W. 1847 wb-9-24

Stewart, Ann 1812 wb-1-277

Stewart, John 1800 wb-1-4

Stewart, John 1840 wb-7-217

Stewart, Thomas 1839 wb-7-83

Still, John 1835 wb-6-63

Still, John P. 1858 wb-12-573

Still, Joseph 1840 wb-7-270

Still, Josiah 1830 wb-4-535

Still, Josiah 1840 wb-7-258

Still, Rebecca 1849 wb-9-272

Stith, Ferdinando 1856 wb-12-46

Stockett, Daniel 1836 wb-6-244

Stockett, Joseph H. 1821 Wb-3-228

Stockett, Joseph H. 1832 wb-5-172

Stockett, Noble 1803 Wb-1-108

Stockett, Thomas W. 1820 wb-3-118

Stokes, Josiah 1830 wb-4-518

Stone, Barton W. 1841 wb-7-377

Stone, Hendley 1834 wb-5-425

Stone, Jane 1828 wb-4-345

Stone, Jane 1829 wb-4-374

Stone, John 1831 wb-5-20

Stone, John H. 1831 wb-5-41

Stone, John H. 1836 wb-6-142

Stone, Mary 1840 wb-7-340

Stone, Sarah A. 1841 wb-7-486

Stone, Sarah Ann 1842 wb-7-529

Stone, William 1812 wb-1-285

Strickland, Joseph 1829 wb-4-465

Strickland, Thomas 1804 Wb-1-131

Stricklin, Joseph 1827 wb-4-157

Stringfellow, William 1816 wb-2-203

Stroud, Ann E. 1853 wb-10-610

Stuart, Thomas 1838 wb-7-6

SuBards, James 1812 wb-1-321

Sudbury, William D. 1836 wb-6-185

Sudbury, William D. 1846 wb-8-399

Sumner, Thomas E. 1817 wb-3-90

Sumner, Thomas E. 1820 wb-3-112

Sumner, Thomas E. 1833 wb-5-283

Swaney, John 1846 wb-8-394

Swanson, Edward 1840 wb-7-342

Swanson, Edward 1843 wb-8-87

Swanson, James 1850 wb-9-426

Swanson, Mary 1845 wb-8-345

Sweet, Moses 1848 wb-9-72

Swipes, John H. 1853 wb-10-462

Swipes, John R. 1853 wb-10-457

Tait, Caleb 1822 wb-3-360

Tapley, John 1809 wb-1-196

Tarkington, Jesse 1834 wb-5-355

Tarkington, Jesse 1836 wb-6-122

Tarkington, William 1833 wb-5-219

Tarkington, William 1836 wb-6-119

Tarpley, William 1828 wb-4-333

Tate, John G. 1831 wb-5-19

Taylor, Abram 1844 wb-8-197

Taylor, Absolem 1815 Wb-2-145

Taylor, Carey J. 1854 wb-11-223

Taylor, Charles 1811 wb-1-257

Taylor, James 1847 wb-8-520

Taylor, James sr. 1834 wb-5-397

Taylor, Richard W. 1854 wb-11-260

Taylor, Thomas 1816 wb-2-205

Taylor, William D. 1852 wb-10-189

Temple, Burrell 1844 wb-8-190

Temple, Elizabeth 1836 wb-6-110

Temple, Thomas B. 1834 wb-5-405

Temple, William 1850 wb-9-591

Temple, William A. 1851 wb-9-669

Templeton, James 1821 Wb-3-270

Tenison, Jerome B. 1852 wb-10-357

Tenison, Jerome R. 1851 wb-10-4

Tenison, Matthew 1850 wb-9-408

Tennison, Washington 1852 wb-10-372

Terrell, Jessee 1852 wb-10-189

Terrill, James 1827 wb-4-162

Terrill, Timothy 1859 wb-13-93

Terry, David 1815 Wb-2-137

Terry, Susan M. 1858 wb-12-486

Thomas, Anthony H. 1815 Wb-2-167

Thomas, James G. 1828 wb-4-336

Thomas, Jesse 1813 Wb-2-78

Thomas, Mark 1816 Wb-2-191

Thomas, William 1841 wb-7-477

Thompson, James 1848 wb-9-67

Thompson, James 1859 wb-13-85

Thompson, John 1859 wb-13-95

Thompson, Robert C. 1832 wb-5-210

Thornton, Burwell 1806 wb-1-191

Thornton, Burwell 1817 wb-2-345

Thurman, Graves 1854 wb-11-188

Thweat, Francis 1820 wb-3-197

Tindall, Henry 1857 wb-12-428

Tomblin, James 1822 wb-3-355

Tomlinson, James 1818 wb-2-363

Toon, James 1839 wb-7-206

Toon, Lewis 1817 wb-2-322

Trantham, John K. 1853 wb-10-464

Trimble, William 1860 wb-13-231

Truett, John 1859 wb-13-246

Trull, Nathan 1817 wb-2-324

Tucker, Allen C. 1856 wb-12-256

Tucker, Willis 1819 wb-3-39

Tulloss, Robert C. 1857 wb-12-323

Tulloss, Rodham 1840 wb-7-305

Tulloss, Rodham 1850 wb-9-341

Turner, Henry 1846 wb-8-408

Turner, James 1835 wb-6-72

Turner, John 1830 wb-4-544

Turner, John J. 1843 wb-8-52

Turner, Lewis 1849 wb-9-250

Turner, Stephen H. 1861 wb-13-499

Vannatta, Christopher 1815 Wb-2-166

Vaughan, Anderson J. 1844 wb-8-178

Vaughan, Robert 1848 wb-9-61

Vaughan, Robert C. 1855 wb-11-461

Vaughn, James 1831 wb-5-77

Vaughn, James 1836 wb-6-182

Vaughn, Richard D. 1840 wb-7-319

Vernon, Green 1861 wb-13-391

Vernon, John D. 1848 wb-9-117

Vernon, Obediah 1831 wb-5-2

Vernon, Richard 1840 wb-7-309

Vernon, Robert 1846 wb-8-486

Wade, Daniel F. 1853 wb-11-30

Wade, Simpson H. 1847 wb-9-9

Wadsworth, Jason 1807 wb-1-171

Waggoner, Alfred T. 1853 wb-10-494

Waggoner, James M. 1853 wb-10-531

Waggoner, Rhoda Ann 1851 wb-9-674

Waggoner, Valentine 1853 wb-10-494

Wakefield, Joseph 1851 wb-10-96

Walker, Freeman 1836 wb-6-154

Walker, Hanch 1815 Wb-2-177

Walker, Henry 1824 wb-3-699

Walker, Henry 1854 wb-11-209

Walker, Joel 1844 wb-8-187

Walker, John 1824 wb-3-721

Walker, John 1843 wb-8-17

Walker, Mary 1853 wb-10-495

Walker, Mary 1855 wb-11-509

Walker, Noah 1827 wb-4-204

Walker, William C. 1857 wb-12-475

Wall, Edmond 1850 wb-9-461

Wall, John E. 1854 wb-11-266

Wall, William W. 1848 wb-9-180

Waller, Alfred 1851 wb-9-658

Waller, John H. 1854 wb-11-404

Waller, Joseph 1850 wb-9-366

Waller, Joseph S. 1842 wb-7-589

Walters, Eli A. 1861 wb-13-398

Walters, Laban 1854 wb-11-258

Walton, George L. 1816 wb-2-243

Walton, Josiah 1816 wb-2-203

Walton, Josiah S. 1819 wb-3-35

Walton, Langhorn T. 1821 Wb-3-246

Ward, Samuel 1831 wb-5-42

Warren, Drury 1852 wb-10-141

Warren, John Sr. 1860 wb-13-377

Warren, Michael 1807 wb-1-174

Warren, Narcissa A. 1853 wb-10-528

Warren, William 1822 wb-3-362

Warren, William 1837 wb-6-429

Waters, John 1840 wb-7-224

Waters, Obediah 1828 wb-4-281

Watkins, Jacob 1836 wb-6-208

Watkins, Nancy 1840 wb-7-278

Watkins, Owen L. 1834 wb-5-379

Watkins, Owen T. 1833 wb-5-287

Watson, B. 0. 1857 wb-12-434

Watson, Jane 1855 wb-12-6

Watson, John 1851 wb-10-120

Watson, John 1851 wb-10-91

Watson, John J. 1845 wb-8-245

Webb, Henry Y. 1836 wb-6-93

Webb, William 1840 wb-7-249

Webb, William L. 1848 wb-9-160

Wells, Betsy 1852 wb-10-386

Wells, John 1816 wb-2-209

West, Elizabeth 1852 wb-10-241

West, Isaac 1841 wb-7-412

West, John 1849 wb-9-275

West, Mary 1856 wb-12-271
Wheaton, Calvin 1818 wb-2-399
Wheaton, Jane 1812 wb-1-322
Wheaton, Jane 1822 wb-3-582
Wheaton, John L. 1834 wb-5-345
Wheaton, Sterling 1823 wb-3-640
White, Abiah 1856 wb-12-115
White, Abner N. 1835 wb-6-48
White, Abram 1839 wb-7-192
White, Benjamin 1827 wb-4-255
White, Benjamin F. 1841 wb-7-459
White, Chapman 1825 wb-3-754
White, Franklin P. 1844 wb-8-208
White, George 1850 wb-9-356
White, Henry 1815 Wb-2-136
White, Holland L. 1838 wb-7-17
White, James C. 1842 wb-7-578
White, John 1825 wb-4-39
White, Martha 1846 wb-8-402
White, Martha M. 1858 wb-12-540
White, Miles 1861 wb-13-479
White, Mordecai 1842 wb-7-548
White, Nancy 1851 wb-10-3
White, Robert 1826 wb-4-72
White, Robert 1840 wb-7-220
White, Robert 1851 wb-10-3
White, Sally 1841 wb-7-485

White, Susan A. 1851 wb-10-151
White, Wiley B. 1860 wb-13-364
White, William 1850 wb-9-431
White, Wilson 1827 wb-4-212
Whitfield, Wilkins 1841 wb-7-444
Whitley, Mary 1824 wb-3-703
Wilburn, F. G. 1838 wb-7-65
Wilburn, Felix G. 1841 wb-7-392
Wilburn, Nicholas 1836 wb-6-111
Wilkes, Daniel 1833 wb-5-320
Wilkes, Daniel 1836 wb-6-183
Wilkins, William 1806 wb-1-16
Wilkins, William 1819 wb-3-55
Wilkinson, William 1831 wb-5-13
Willett, Richard 1813 wb-1-336
Williams, Berry P. 1857 wb-12-446
Williams, Diana 1838 wb-6-472
Williams, Elijah 1856 wb-12-70
Williams, Ephraim C. 1832 wb-5-198
Williams, Henry 1852 wb-10-370
Williams, James 1832 wb-5-198
Williams, James R. 1846 wb-8-516
Williams, James W. 1847 wb-8-572
Williams, John 1859 wb-13-94

Williams, Littleberry 1853 wb-10-548

Williams, Samuel 1834 wb-5-381

Williams, Thomas 1835 wb-6-21

Williams, Wiley 1839 wb-7-209

Williams, William 1824 wb-3-739

Williams, William 1858 wb-12-611

Williams, Willis 1840 wb-7-249

Williamson, Henry C. 1831 wb-5-3

Williamson, James 1852 wb-10-373

Williamson, John G. 1831 wb-5-49

Williamson, Martha 1828 wb-4-358

Williamson, Richard 1852 wb-10-263

Williamson, Robert 1820 wb-3-197

Williamson, Thomas 1816 wb-2-252

Willis, George 1846 wb-8-494

Wills, Thomas sr. 1821 Wb-3-259

Wilson, Henrietta 1828 wb-4-300

Wilson, Isaac B. 1861 wb-13-425

Wilson, James 1826 wb-4-137

Wilson, James sr. 1838 wb-6-516

Wilson, Jane 1853 wb-11-35

Wilson, John 1827 wb-4-174

Wilson, John 1853 wb-11-1

Wilson, John L. 1851 wb-9-717

Wilson, John S. 1848 wb-9-206

Wilson, John S. 1859 wb-13-301

Wilson, Joseph 1823 wb-3-650

Wilson, Josiah 1857 wb-12-322

Wilson, Margaret 1828 wb-4-321

Wilson, Mark 1840 wb-7-223

Wilson, Robert 1819 wb-3-95

Wilson, Robert 1835 wb-6-79

Wilson, Samuel 1812 wb-1-305

Wilson, Samuel 1812 wb-2-18

Wilson, Samuel 1822 wb-3-309

Wilson, Samuel D. 1855 wb-11-582

Wilson, Samuel J. 1851 wb-10-325

Wilson, Samuel S. 1854 wb-11-134

Wilson, Thomas 1818 wb-2-377

Wilson, Thomas 1828 wb-4-310

Wilson, Thomas 1852 wb-10-385

Wilson, Zaccheus 1842 wb-7-588

Wimpee, Tyre 1818 wb-2-393

Windrow, Richard 1806 wb-1-24

Winset, Anias 1838 wb-6-464

Winsett, Amos 1836 wb-6-197

Winsett, Robert 1812 wb-1-325

Winsett, Robert 1823 wb-3-649

York, Matilda 1846 wb-8-483
Young, Elizabeth 1819 wb-3-13
Young, James B. 1843 wb-8-
123
Zachary, Benjamin 1858 wb-
12-610
Zachary, William 1859 wb-13-
50
Zachary, William C. 1836 wb-
6-91
Zackery, Mary 1859 wb-13-94

www.ingramcontent.com/pod-product-compliance
Lightning Source LLC
Chambersburg PA
CBHW060557100426
42742CB00013B/2597